JET Library

Joint Education & Training Library

Esse
Den

Mary Mos

Helen Frar

Gayna Sm

D1494368

© 2005 PASTEST Ltd

Egerton Court
Parkgate Estate
Knutsford
Cheshire
WA16 8DX

Telephone: 01565 752000

First published 2005

ISBN: 1 904627 55 2

A catalogue record for this book is available from the British Library.

The information contained within this book was obtained by the authors from reliable sources. However, while every effort has been made to ensure its accuracy, no responsibility for loss, damage or injury occasioned to any person acting or refraining from action as a result of information contained herein can be accepted by the publishers or authors.

Every effort has been made to contact holders of copyright to obtain permission to reproduce copyright material. However, if any have been inadvertently overlooked, the publisher will be pleased to make the necessary arrangements at the first opportunity.

PasTest Revision Books and Intensive Courses

PasTest has been established in the field of postgraduate medical education since 1972, providing revision books and intensive study courses for doctors preparing for their professional examinations.

Books and courses are available for the following specialties:

MRCP Part 1 and 2, MRCPCH Part 1 and 2, MRCGP, MRCPsych, MRCS, MRCOG, DRCOG, DCH, FRCA, PLAB, medical students, NVQ 2 and 3 Veterinary Nursing

For further details contact:

PasTest, Egerton Court, Parkgate Estate, Knutsford, Cheshire WA16 8DX

Tel: 01565 752000   Fax: 01565 650264

Website: www.pastest.co.uk   Email: enquiries@pastest.co.uk

Text prepared by Carnegie Book Production, Lancaster

Printed and bound in Europe by the Alden Group

Contents

About the Authors

Mary Moss

Mary qualified at Manchester Dental Hospital, where she then worked as a qualified dental nurse for five years. She worked part-time in general practice, and spent a further two years working as a dental nurse in the Orthodontic Department at the Royal Bolton Hospital. For the past 10 years she has been employed by a training provider, originally as a scheme coordinator for the National Certificate in Dental Nursing training programme and in later years as a tutor, assessor and internal verifier on the NVQ Levels 2 and 3 in Oral Healthcare.

Helen Franks

Helen qualified as a dental nurse in 1980. She has worked in general dental practices, hospitals and primarily community dental services for 23 years, prior to achieving qualifications in Dental Health Education, Dental Radiography, Dental Sedation and Advanced Life Support for Dental Nurses. Since 2000 Helen has worked as an NVQ dental nurse assessor, tutor and more recently as an internal verifier. She currently teaches the NVQ Level 3 in Oral Healthcare, as well as the Oral Health Education postgraduate course.

Gayna Smith

Gayna qualified from Manchester Dental
Hospital in 1992. Since then she has
gained qualifications in Oral Health
Education and Dental Radiography. She
currently works full time in a private
dental practice in the north west of
England and is also a part-time dental
nurse tutor, assessor and internal verifier
for the NVQ in Oral Healthcare. Gayna
graduated from Bolton Institute in 2003
with a Certificate in Education.

Acknowledgements

We would like to thank the following people for their help, guidance and support:

Michael Cahill of Cahill Dental Care Centre, Bolton

Steven Lomas and the staff at St Andrews Dental Centre, Bury

David Harper and the staff at DM Harper and Associates, Bolton

Judith Anthony BDS

Photographs by
Debra Moss

Introduction

This book has been written by tutors who are at present delivering the NVQ Oral Healthcare Level 2 and Level 3 awards. Each chapter of the book is linked to the units of the Level 3 qualification and is designed to cover the knowledge specification of each unit. This will enable candidates to acquire sufficient knowledge and understanding of the material. Photographs, diagrams and charts have been included throughout the book to support the text.

Although the book is predominantly designed for those candidates undertaking the Oral Healthcare Level 3 award, is also be a good source of knowledge for people embarking on the National Certificate in Dental Nursing or the Access to Registration course. The book is also a valuable source of information to employers who are supporting their employees through dental nurse training.

1 What is an NVQ?

1: What is an NVQ?

Getting started

What is an NVQ?

The letters 'NVQ' stand for *National Vocational Qualification*. NVQs are nationally recognised qualifications in the UK, provided by national training organisations and sector skills councils, who develop National Occupational Standards for each occupational area.

How do I get an NVQ?

To gain the NVQ Level 3 in Oral Healthcare you will need to prove that you have the necessary skills and knowledge and can apply them to a range of workplace situations in order to be judged as competent.

You will need to show that you can carry out your duties, and know **why** you have to carry out these duties, in agreed ways. To gain the NVQ Level 3 in Oral Healthcare you will need to pass an **independent assessment**, set by the National Examining Board for Dental Nurses, and produce a **portfolio** of work-based evidence, to prove competence in your day-to-day workplace duties.

What is my NVQ award made up of?

The Oral Healthcare NVQ award is made up of a set number of units. Some units have to be done by everyone and are known as **mandatory units** and some may be chosen and are known as **optional units**. Optional units must be selected to reflect your day-to-day workplace duties, matching your own work role. Each named unit has been designed to represent an area of a dental nurse's role, within a variety of dental procedures.

What is a unit?

A unit is made up of a number of **elements** (different parts of an overall task). In order to show competence for this unit, you need to complete all the elements of each unit. Each element lists **performance criteria** (which describe how you have to do the task), a **range** (the different situations or aspects of the task that must be covered) and **knowledge** (identifies what you need to know and understand to complete the task).

What evidence do I need for my portfolio and how will I get it?

All candidates need to prepare a portfolio with different types of evidence. Your portfolio will be unique to you and will represent your duties within your own workplace. You will need to prove that you can perform certain tasks by providing evidence for your portfolio. Your **assessor** will give you suggestions about the suitable types of evidence required to show competence for each element of each unit of the qualification.

Who will be included in my NVQ award?

The candidate – You! While you are in the process of gaining your NVQ you will be referred to as the 'Candidate'.

The assessor – A qualified dental nurse or dentist who has also gained D.32, D.33 or A1, A2 Assessor award, qualifying them to plan, review and make judgements about your competence.

The tutor – A qualified dental nurse or dentist, who has also gained a teaching qualification. They will deliver a series of agreed classes or one-to-one tutorials, covering the information relating to each unit of the qualification. This will enable you to gain greater understanding of your duties and responsibilities in your day-to-day work.

The workplace manager/employer – A person who will support you for the duration of your NVQ programme, by allowing work-based observation to take place, supplying you with witness testimonies (see next section), and identifying and removing any barriers to your progress within your workplace.

The internal verifier – A person who advises both you and your assessor, as well as checking your evidence and that each assessment has been carried out properly.

The external verifier – Persons approved and appointed by City and Guilds to make sure that the centre where you are undergoing your training maintains high standards of delivery and adheres to the NVQ Code of Practice.

The quality assurance manager – Each training centre has a person who is responsible for ensuring that the centre works in accordance with City and Guilds' requirements.

How is evidence generated?

Direct observation – Being watched by an assessor while completing tasks in the workplace.

Witness testimony – Written statement supplied by a suitably qualified member of staff on how a task is performed.

Written and verbal questioning – Tests your knowledge and understanding underlying your performance.

Simulation – This may be carried out when a naturally occurring observation is not possible, eg role-play.

Case study/role-play – An in-depth study of a particular situation or patient.

Accreditation of prior learning – A relevant qualification, which has been gained before the one that you are taking, eg if you complete NVQ in Oral Healthcare Support Level 2 you are exempt from DNO 1 and 2 in Level 3.

Professional discussion – A written account of a discussion between yourself and your assessor about a particular subject or scenario.

Personal statement – A statement written by yourself about something that you have achieved or your opinion about a situation.

Independent assessment – This NVQ requires the candidate to sit a formal written test known as the independent assessment.

Candidate induction

At the beginning of your dental nursing training you may be required to attend a 'course induction'. The aims of the induction are to:

- inform you about all those people who will be involved in your assessment and what their different roles will be

- ensure that you know about your assessment centre and what you can expect from your tutor, assessor, internal verifier, centre manager and external verifier.

- inform you how your Oral Healthcare NVQ will be assessed and what you have the right to expect

- inform you what to do if 'things go wrong'

- inform you about the structure of the award
- inform you how to identify, submit and organise the evidence that you submit in your portfolio.

The induction may also allow you to take an assessment to identify any additional support that you may require to achieve the qualification.

As an NVQ candidate the 'Access to Complaints' and 'Appeals Process' should be fully explained to you. It allows you, as the Candidate, the opportunity to appeal if you feel that judgements made by your assessor about your competency or the assessment methods used were unfair or unsuitable.

KEY TERMS

Unit	A group of related specific skills or work tasks
Element	One specific task or skill within the unit
Performance criteria	How a task is to be undertaken
Evidence	Proof that all assessment requirements are met; the evidence will include records of observations, oral and written questions, and witness testimonies
Assessment	The process whereby your assessor considers the evidence produced and judges it against the performance criteria, range and knowledge of each unit of the qualification

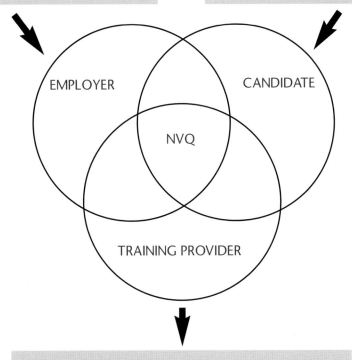

Understands complete NVQ format and 'Standards'

Provides witness testimonies

Encourages students to attend college – if required by training provider

Available to sign/date paperwork when required

Completes portfolio of evidence, in time available

Regularly attends college, if required by the training provider

Successfully achieves written assessments

Participates in workplace observations

EMPLOYER

CANDIDATE

NVQ

TRAINING PROVIDER

Provides underpinning knowledge

Assesses through observations and/or simulation if appropriate

Provides guidance and support throughout qualification to complete all requirements as written in the Standards

Fig. 1.1 Algorithm of the training programme for achieving the Oral Healthcare NVQ Level 3 award.

Employers' guide

Employers have a very important role in their employees' training. It is important that, as an employer, you are aware of the course your dental nurse is undertaking and what the assessment requirements are (see section 'What is an NVQ?', page 4). It is advisable to look at the NVQ standards so that you know what subjects are to be covered during the course. The person providing the training should give these to your employee at the beginning of the course.

It is the responsibility of employers, or delegated suitably qualified members of staff, to act as mentors to help guide employees through their work role to meet the requirements of the NVQ. During the NVQ, as the employer, you will need to:

- give support and encouragement to your employees

- liaise with their assessors

- provide witness testimonies to say that they are competent in various dental procedures

- allow assessors to carry out work-based observations in the dental surgery (this will involve them being present in the dental surgery while the dental nurse works but they will be as unobtrusive as possible)

- be available to give written and verbal comments about how your employee is progressing in the workplace.

The cost of the course varies depending on the training provider. Funding is available from your local learning and skills council. The NVQ is different from the National Examination as it involves a lot of work-based support, employer commitment and constant assessment throughout the course. The National Examination is based on a written exam, spotter, mixing and oral exam all taken in one day. It does not involve any evidence of work-based products.

The dental nurse's role

A dental nurse, along with dental hygienists, therapists and technicians, works as part of the dental team. All these professionals are also known as Dental Care Professionals (DCPs). It is the dental nurse's role to ensure the smooth running of the dental surgery by assisting the dentist during a variety of clinical procedures and making sure that the patient is comfortable throughout. A dental nurse's duties vary depending on where they work, but the main duties for any dental nurse are to:

- adhere to health and safety policies
- maintain a high level of cross-infection control
- ensure that instruments and equipment are available and sterilised for use
- mix a variety of materials and medicaments at the correct consistency and amount required
- have a good knowledge of the dental profession, dental diseases and the methods of prevention.

Some dental nurses also undertake reception duties such as answering the telephone, making appointments, filing and handling money.

Certain skills and attributes are required to be an efficient dental nurse. These are:

- being a good communicator
- being a good listener
- ability to be very organised
- clean and tidy presentation
- punctuality
- having a sympathetic nature
- having the ability to work as part of a team.

Patients see the dental nurse as someone who is there not only to assist the dentist but also to look after them and act as a communicator between themselves and the dentist. Patients usually feel more comfortable about asking the dental nurse or receptionist questions about their treatment. As a dental nurse, you should be prepared for this, and it is very important that you give the patient the correct information. If you are unsure about the information that you should give to a patient never guess. Always seek confirmation from another team member or refer the patient to someone who knows more than you do. Common questions that a patient may ask are:

- Will it hurt?
- How much will it cost?
- What is involved with my treatment?
- How do I look after my denture/brace?

It is important that you never try to explain anything to a patient that you know nothing about.

A dental nurse is not permitted to carry out any procedure that is classed as the practising of dentistry, as outlined in section 37(1) of the Dentists Act 1984. In view of the new statutory registration, which is imminent, the General Dental Council (GDC) is expected to start registering dental nurses in July 2006. In the light of this, the Voluntary National Register of Dental Nurses will close to any new members on 31 December 2005. The GDC has also published the *Standards for Dental Professionals*, which came into effect on 1 June 2005. These are the standards that all dental professionals are expected to abide by, including dental nurses. The British Association of Dental Nurses has adopted these standards, and these have replaced the original code of ethics. The standards outlined by the GDC are:

- Protect patients' interests and ensure that they are a priority
- Respect patients' rights and their right to choice
- Maintain confidentiality
- Work with other members of the dental team in the interests of patients
- Continue to update knowledge and professional development
- Be trusted by patients and fellow colleagues.

For the latest information on Statutory Registration visit the GDC website (www.gdc-uk.org).

2 Biology and Anatomy

2: Biology and Anatomy

Circulatory system

The heart

The heart and blood vessels are part of the circulatory system. The heart is a fist-sized pump and has arteries, which are blood vessels that carry blood away from the heart (Fig. 2.1), and veins, which carry blood to the heart from the rest of the body. Thus the blood circulates, carrying oxygen and nutrients.

There are four separate chambers in the heart: two atria and two ventricles. The atria receive blood returning to the heart and the ventricles pump the blood out from the heart. Each of these chambers has a one-way valve to ensure that the blood flow is always in one direction. With each beat, the right ventricle pumps de-oxygenated blood to the lungs while the left ventricle pumps oxygenated blood to the rest of the body. This happens approximately 2.5 billion times in an average lifetime.

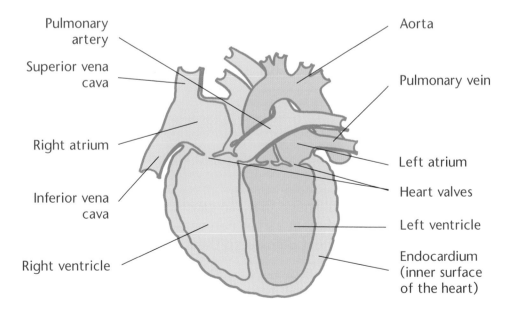

Pulmonary artery

Superior vena cava

Right atrium

Inferior vena cava

Right ventricle

Aorta

Pulmonary vein

Left atrium

Heart valves

Left ventricle

Endocardium (inner surface of the heart)

Fig. 2.1 The four chambers of the heart and the blood vessels that lead out of and into the heart.

Oxygenation of the blood

The red blood cells are responsible for the oxygenation of the blood, which takes place in the lungs. The veins carry blood back to the heart, which then sends it to the lung for re-oxygenation. Oxygen from the air inhaled into the lungs is transported in the red blood cells back to the heart. From the heart, the oxygenated blood is carried to all parts of the body by the arteries.

Blood

Constituents of blood

- Erythrocytes (red blood cells)
- Thrombocytes (blood platelets)
- Leucocytes (white blood cells)
- Plasma — associated with defence mechanisms, such as blood clotting and antibody production.

Problems with the blood

There are several blood-related diseases. Those that are most relevant to dental nurses are:

- Hepatitis B
- Acquired immune deficiency syndrome (AIDS)/human immunodeficiency virus (HIV) infection
- Sickle cell disease
- Anaemia
- Haemophilia
- Thalassaemias.

Hepatitis B is a serious illness, that can cause chronic fatigue, loss of appetite, fever and jaundice. In a small percentage of patients, the disease can cause permanent damage to the liver.

HIV/AIDS is a blood-borne disease that affects the immune system, making the affected individual highly susceptible to life-threatening infections, such as pneumonia. HIV has been found in blood, semen, saliva, tears, nervous system tissue, breast milk and female genital tract secretions. However, only blood, semen, female genital tract secretions and breast milk have been proved to transmit HIV to others. The infection is more commonly spread by illicit intravenous drug usage and/or sexual intercourse.

Sickle cell disease is a hereditary blood disease resulting from a single amino acid mutation of the red blood cells. People with sickle cell disease have red blood cells that contain mostly haemoglobin S, an abnormal type of haemoglobin. Sometimes the red blood cells become crescent shaped (sickle shaped) and have difficulty passing through small blood vessels. There is currently no universal cure for blood-borne sickle cell disease.

Anaemia is a disorder that is caused by an acquired or inherited reduction in the number of red blood cells in the blood. The red blood cells carry oxy-haemoglobin to the body tissues. Iron deficiency is a sign of anaemia. Symptoms of anaemia include tiredness, ulcers, palpitations, thrush, dizziness, headache, fainting, and difficulty in sleeping and concentration. There are different types of anaemia.

Aplastic anaemia is a rare condition in which the bone marrow produces insufficient blood cells for the patient's circulation. It is not a type of cancer. Symptoms include red and bleeding gums, blood blisters in the mouth, recurrent sore throats, petechial rash (commonly a sign in meningitis) and high incidence of infection.

Haemophilia is a genetic blood disease in which the blood is unable to form a firm clot normally and quickly. This is an important disease to be aware of in the dental surgery, as bleeding can occur after dental treatment, particularly extractions and deep scaling.

The thalassaemias are a group of genetic blood disorders. The World Health Organization (WHO) recognises thalassaemia as the most prevalent inherited blood disorder in the world. The predominant areas where thalassaemia occurs are the Mediterranean, Middle East, India, South East Asia, and also include Southern China.

Respiratory system

The hairs in the nose act as a filter when we inhale. The inhaled air flows into the trachea, which ends in two short branches called bronchi (Fig. 2.2). The bronchi branch into smaller bunches of tubes called bronchioles, and further down are tiny sac-like clusters called alveoli, which are designed to let oxygen diffuse through their thin walls. Oxygen exchange takes place between the alveoli and the surrounding capillaries.

The epiglottis is a small flap of tissue that helps prevent food from entering the lungs via the trachea. The diaphragm is a large sheet of muscle beneath the lungs, and this moves with every breath to help move the air in and out of the body.

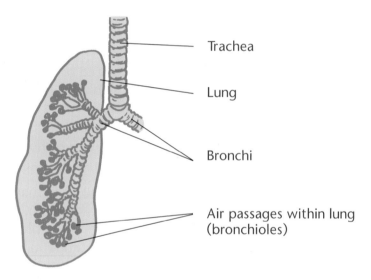

Trachea

Lung

Bronchi

Air passages within lung
(bronchioles)

Fig. 2.2 The trachea and its branches, and the lung.

Breathing consists of two phases, inspiration and expiration. During **inspiration**, the diaphragm and the intercostal muscles contract. The diaphragm moves downwards increasing the volume of the chest cavity. The intercostal muscles then pull the ribs up. This expands the ribcage, further increasing this volume within the lungs. The air within the lungs rushes in through the respiratory tract and into the alveoli. The alveoli are tiny sac-like clusters as described above. In contrast to inspiration, during **expiration** the diaphragm and intercostal muscles relax. This increases the air pressure in the lungs, forcing the air out.

External respiration

When a breath is taken, air passes in through the nostrils, through the nasal passages into the pharynx, then through the larynx and down the trachea, into one of the main bronchi. There are smaller bronchial tubules through which the air will pass, and on towards even smaller bronchioles, into a microscopic air sac called the alveolus. It is here that external respiration occurs. This is caused by the exchange of oxygen and carbon dioxide between the air and the blood in the lungs.

Digestive system

The 7.6 metre (25 foot) digestive system (from mouth to anus) begins in the oral cavity. Ptyalin is a digestive enzyme that is responsible for the first stage of digestion, and acts during mastication of the food. The enzyme is produced by the salivary glands and breaks starches down into smaller molecules. After the food has been chewed and swallowed it travels down the oesophagus. This is a long tube that runs from the mouth down to the stomach. Peristalsis, or wave-like motion, helps transport the food downwards. This helps us digest food when we are upright and even when we are upside down.

Once in the stomach, the food is digested further by gastric acid. The stomach is a large expandable sac-like organ that churns and bathes the food. After digestion has taken place in the stomach, the food travels further down into the duodenum (the first part of the small intestine) and then into the ileum (the final part of the intestine). Inside the small intestine, bile (see below) helps the further breakdown of food, which is mixed with pancreatic and other digestive enzymes to aid digestion.

The waste is transported down to the large intestine. Here some of the water is removed, as well as some of the electrolytes (such as sodium). *Lactobacillus acidophilus* and *Escherichia coli*, which are naturally present in the large intestine, further aid the digestion process. Waste travels along the ascending colon, the transverse colon and then the sigmoid colon. The journey finally ends at the anus – the whole process from consumption to faecal waste being released taking approximately 24 hours. So while you are eating breakfast today, you are in the final stages of digesting yesterday's breakfast!

The pancreas is made up of two glands: the exocrine and endocrine glands. The exocrine gland produces some enzymes which enter the duodenum via the pancreatic duct. The endocrine gland partially produces insulin, which regulates the blood sugar.

The liver produces bile, which is a watery greenish fluid. The bile travels along the hepatic duct into the gallbladder, where it is stored. Bile contains bile salts, bile pigments (bilirubin, which is the non-iron part of haemoglobin), phospholipids and cholesterol. When gallstones are produced, they are usually cholesterol based, and cause extreme pain, raised temperature, jaundice and general illness when they block the hepatic or common bile ducts.

Tongue

The tongue (Fig 2.3) is a muscle attached to the floor of the mouth. It is used for speech and swallowing. The tongue is covered with a variety of papillae, which detect different tastes.

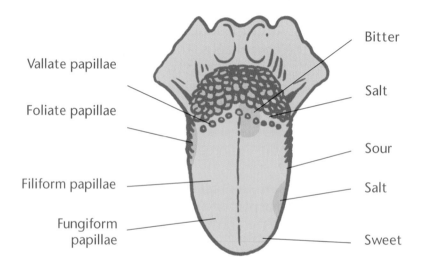

Fig. 2.3 The tongue with the various papillae. Different tastes are detected in different parts of the tongue.

Saliva

Saliva has many functions:

- Lubrication
- Cleansing
- Buffering (neutralising acid)
- Aiding digestion

- Remineralisation
- Protection (against oral infections).

Saliva is composed of water, proteins, sodium, chloride, bicarbonate, calcium and phosphate. The water lubricates and cleanses, the bicarbonate neutralises plaque acid, and the calcium and phosphate help remineralise early carious lesions.

The average amount of saliva an adult produces in a day is 500 ml. Some people do not produce enough saliva and have a condition known as dry mouth or xerostomia. Certain prescribed medicines or some medical conditions such as Sjögren's syndrome can cause dry mouth. Saliva is produced by three pairs of salivary glands in the mouth. These are called the parotid, sublingual and submandibular glands (Fig. 2.4).

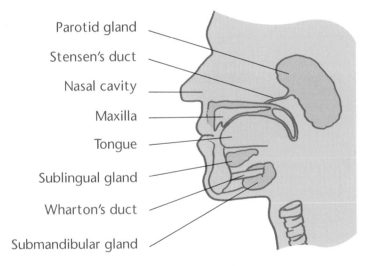

Parotid gland
Stensen's duct
Nasal cavity
Maxilla
Tongue
Sublingual gland
Wharton's duct
Submandibular gland

Fig. 2.4 The three main salivary glands and their ducts.

The parotid gland is the largest salivary gland and opens into the mouth via Stensen's duct opposite the upper molar teeth. This gland is affected in mumps. The submandibular gland lies next to the body of the mandible and opens into the mouth via Wharton's duct, which opens beneath the tongue. The sublingual gland lies under the tongue. It has several ducts, which open under the tongue where the saliva flows onto the lingual surfaces of the lower incisors.

KEY TERMS

Heart

Heart	A cone-shaped hollow muscle found just beneath the breast bone in your chest. It is about the size of your fist
Aorta	The largest blood vessel in the body, which carries oxgenated blood to every part of the body; it receives its blood from the left-hand side of the heart (left ventricle)
Arteries	Carry blood away **from the heart**
Veins	Carry blood **towards** the heart
Capillaries	Very small blood vessels that supply the tissues with blood
Septum	The dividing partition that separates the left and right sides of the heart; the septum is also divided into two parts
Superior vena cava	Returns blood black to the right atrium from the upper part of the body; it is one of the largest veins in the body
Inferior vena cava	Carries blood back to the right atrium from the lower parts of the body
Pulmonary arteries	Carry blood from the right ventricle to both lungs ... it is then oxygenated and sent to the left atrium of the heart
Pulmonary veins	Carry oxygenated blood back to the left atrium in the heart

Digestive system

Submandibular glands	Pair of salivary glands that are situated at the angles of the mandible; they produce saliva which emerges from just under the tongue
Sublingual glands	Lie on either side of the tongue, producing saliva that will also emerge from several ducts underneath the tongue

Parotid glands	The largest salivary glands that lie in front of the ears, and make up around 25% of the saliva, which travels along the parotid ducts, and emerges near the upper molar teeth
Ptyalin	Digestive enzyme in the saliva, making chewing (mastication) the first stage of digestion by working at the same time
Peristalsis	Wave-like motion that transports food down the digestive tract
Oesophagus	A tube (approximately 23cm long) that is the first part of the digestive tract, connected to the oral cavity
Stomach	C-shaped organ on the left-hand side of the body (the liver is on the right side); the stomach secretes both mucus and acid and is used temporarily to store food, and churn and digest into a smoother substance (chyme) before passing it down to the small intestine
Duodenum	First part of the small intestine which secretes enzymes; ulcers are commonly formed here, as stomach acid can squirt back to this point
Small intestine	Composed of the jejunum and ileum (about 6 m in total); food passes down through it, and this contains further undigested food residue, which is rich in bacteria
Large intestine	Reabsorbs water, then eliminates the waste as faeces from the anus
Pancreas	A two-part gland that is partly responsible for producing insulin
Liver	The organ that lies to the right of the stomach and produces bile
Gallbladder	The organ that stores bile once it has been produced by the liver

Regional anatomy

Skull (Figs 2.5 and 2.6)

See Fig. 2.5. The frontal, parietal, occipital and temporal bones are all plates that make up the skull. They are joined together by the coronal sutures.

Fig. 2.5 The skull - anatomy.

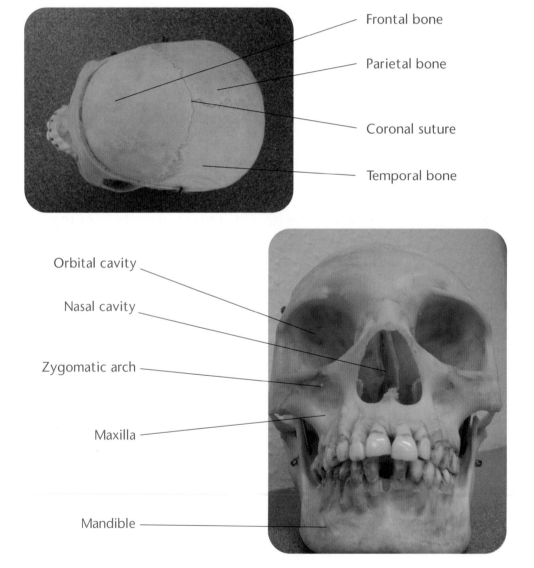

Frontal bone

Parietal bone

Coronal suture

Temporal bone

Orbital cavity

Nasal cavity

Zygomatic arch

Maxilla

Mandible

Fig. 2.6 Front view of the skull showing the zygomatic arches (cheekbones), nasal cavities, orbital cavities, mandible and maxilla.

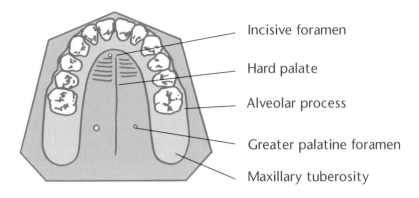

- Incisive foramen
- Hard palate
- Alveolar process
- Greater palatine foramen
- Maxillary tuberosity

Fig. 2.7 Palatal view of the maxilla showing the incisive and greater palatine foramina – where the nerves and blood supply run through to supply the teeth.

Jaws

The upper jaw is called the maxilla (see Fig. 2.5). The maxilla is made up of two halves of bone that join at the midline. The upper jaw holds the upper teeth in place inside the alveolar processes. The maxilla forms the roof of the mouth – the hard palate (Fig. 2.6) – and the floor of the nose. There are also hollow spaces inside the top of the maxilla called the sinuses (maxillary antrum).

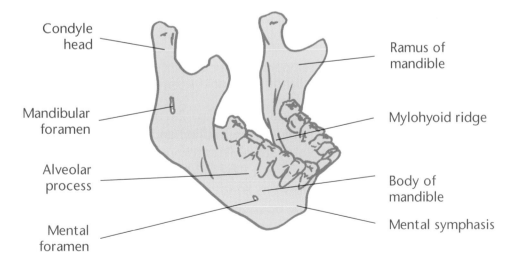

- Condyle head
- Mandibular foramen
- Alveolar process
- Mental foramen
- Ramus of mandible
- Mylohyoid ridge
- Body of mandible
- Mental symphasis

Fig. 2.8 Parts of the mandible.

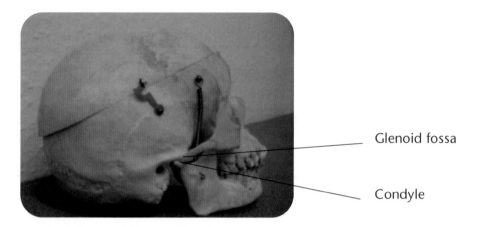

Fig. 2.9 The temporomandibular joint.

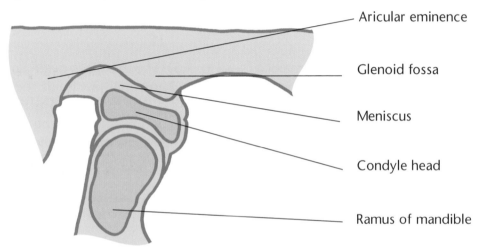

Fig. 2.10 Cross-section of the temporomandibular joint showing the articular disc between the condylar head and the glenoid fossa.

The lower jaw is called the mandible (see Figs 2.6 and 2.8). This is also formed of two halves, which join at the midline and hold the lower teeth in place. Nerves and blood supply run through the mandibular and mental foramina to supply the teeth. The lower jaw is connected to the upper jaw by a hinge joint known as the temporomandibular joint (TMJ). These joints enable the jaws to open and close, allowing them to perform functions such as eating and talking.

The condyle of the mandible sits against the temporal bone in a groove called the glenoid fossa (Fig. 2.8). A cartilage separates the two bones so that they do not grate against each other (Fig. 2.9). Sometimes the condyle can dislocate: this is known as TMJ dysfunction.

Muscles of mastication

These are the group of muscles that help to open and close the mouth and help us to chew (Fig 2.10a and b).

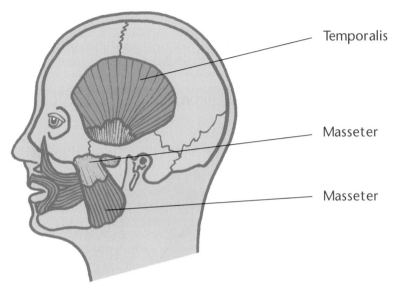

Temporalis

Masseter

Masseter

Fig. 2.10a

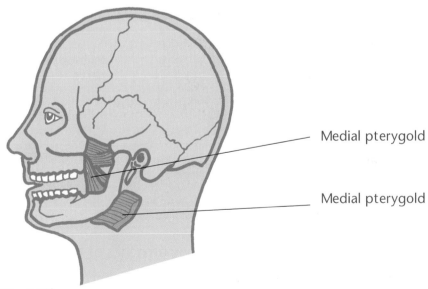

Medial pterygold

Medial pterygold

Fig. 2.10b

Fig. 2.10a and 2.10b The muscles of mastication.

Nerve supply to the teeth

The nerve supply to the teeth and surrounding structures comes from the cranial nerves, which emerge from the brain. Nerves can be either sensory – to feel stimuli – or motor – for movement. Cranial nerves occur in pairs and only the following four of the 12 pairs of cranial nerves are relevant to dentistry:

- Cranial nerve V (trigeminal nerve)
- Cranial nerve VII (facial nerve)
- Cranial nerve IX (glossopharyngeal nerve)
- Cranial nerve XII (hypoglossal nerve)

Trigeminal nerve

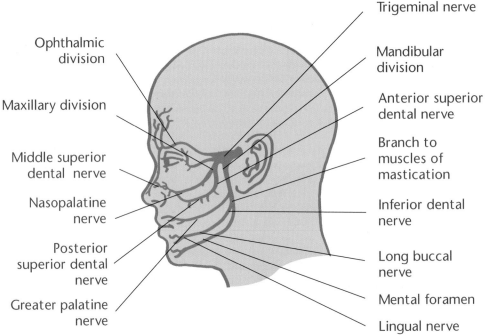

Ophthalmic division

Maxillary division

Middle superior dental nerve

Nasopalatine nerve

Posterior superior dental nerve

Greater palatine nerve

Trigeminal nerve

Mandibular division

Anterior superior dental nerve

Branch to muscles of mastication

Inferior dental nerve

Long buccal nerve

Mental foramen

Lingual nerve

Fig. 2.12 The trigeminal nerve, its divisions and further branches.

This nerve splits into three divisions with many branches of the nerve running from them.

Ophthalmic division – This supplies the soft tissue around the eyes and the upper part of the face.

Maxillary division – This has five branches, which supply the upper teeth and the maxilla. The anterior superior dental nerve supplies the incisors and canines and the labial gingivae. The middle superior dental nerve supplies the premolars and the mesial portion of the first molar teeth and the buccal gingivae. The posterior superior dental nerve supplies the distal portion of the first molar, all other molars and their buccal gingivae. The greater palatine nerve supplies the distal portion of the canine palatal gingivae and the palatal gingivae of the premolars and molars. The nasopalatine nerve (formerly known as the long sphenopalatine nerve) supplies the palatal gingivae of the incisors and the mesial portion of palatal gingivae around the canines.

Mandibular division – This has four branches that supply the lower teeth and the mandible, and there is a motor branch to the muscles of mastication. The inferior dental nerve supplies all the lower teeth, the buccal gingivae up to the premolars, the lip and the chin. The lingual nerve supplies all the lingual gingivae and the floor of the mouth. The long buccal nerve supplies the buccal gingivae of the molar teeth. The motor nerve to the muscles of mastication enables movement of these muscles.

Facial nerve

This supplies the sublingual and submandibular salivary glands and enables the movement of the muscles of facial expression. This nerve also enables the taste sensation to occur on the anterior two-thirds of the tongue.

Glossopharyngeal nerve

This supplies the parotid salivary gland and allows the muscles at the back of the mouth to work. This nerve also enables the taste sensation to occur at the back of the tongue.

Hypoglossal nerve

This nerve allows movement of the tongue.

Structure of a tooth (Fig. 2.13) and its supporting structures (Fig. 2.14)

Teeth sit in the jaw bones and are anchored by roots that cannot be seen by just looking in the mouth. The part of a tooth that is seen in the mouth is called the crown. Teeth are of various shapes and sizes, and vary in the number of cusps and roots that they have. The composition of all teeth (their structure) is the same.

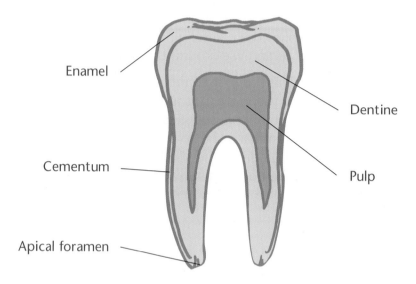

Fig. 2.13 Structure of a tooth.

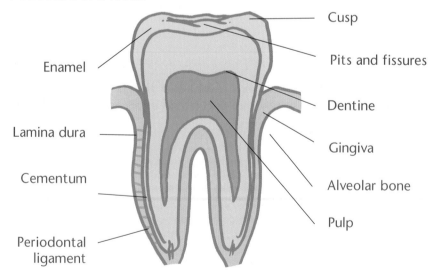

Fig. 2.14 Cross-section through a tooth and its supporting structures.

Enamel

This is the hardest substance in the body and is made up of enamel prisms, which are 96% made up of a mineral called hydroxyapatite. Enamel alone does not experience sensitivity as it has no nerve supply. The junction where the enamel sits next to the dentine is called the dentinoenamel junction. Enamel covers the tooth from the biting surface down to the gingival crevice.

Dentine

This is much softer than enamel and forms the bulk of any tooth and also gives the tooth its colour. It is made up of dentine tubules. Unlike enamel, the dentine is sensitive. When dentine becomes damaged it can be repaired through the formation of secondary dentine by odontoblasts, which are found in the pulp chamber.

Cementum

This covers the dentine on the root of the tooth so it will not normally be visible in the mouth.

Pulp

This contains the nerves and blood supply to a tooth, which enter the tooth through the apical foramen at the apex of the root. The pulp (when vital) allows the tooth to feel stimuli such as hot, cold and pain.

Gingiva

When healthy, the gingiva has a pink and stippled appearance and is tight against the tooth, leaving a slight 2 mm crevice at the neck. The gingiva covers the bone and the root of the tooth (which is in the bony socket).

Periodontal ligament

This attaches the tooth in the socket to the alveolar bone. It acts as a shock absorber so that the tooth moves slightly during eating.

Alveolar bone

This is the bone in which the teeth sit in the jaw. It is an extension of both the maxilla and the mandible. The outer layer of bone is hard and compact but the inner layer is spongier. The outside surface of the bone is called the lamina dura.

Development of the dentition

Development of the deciduous dentition begins when a baby is still developing in the womb. Calcification of these teeth begins during the fourth month in the fetus, and, by the end of the sixth month, all of the deciduous teeth have begun to calcify. The complete set of deciduous teeth erupts by around 2.5 years of age (Table 2.1), by which time the permanent dentition has begun calcification.

Table 2.1 Eruption times of teeth

TOOTH	DECIDUOUS	PERMANENT
Upper jaw		
Central incisor	8–12 months	7–8 years
Lateral incisor	9–13 months	8–9 years
Canine	16–22 months	11–12 years
First premolar		10–11 years
Second premolar		10–12 years
First molar	13–19 months	6–7 years
Second molar	25–33 months	12–13 years
Third molar		17–21 years
Lower jaw		
Central incisor	6–10 months	6–7 years
Lateral incisor	10–16 months	7–8 years
Canine	17–23 months	9–10 years
First premolar		11–12 years
Second premolar		10–12 years
First molar	14–18 months	6–7 years
Second molar	23–31 months	10–12 years
Third molar		17–21 years

Surfaces of the tooth

Mesial – the surface of the tooth facing towards the middle of the mouth.

Distal – surface of a tooth facing towards the back of the mouth.

Occlusal – the top surface of the tooth that is used as the biting surface.

Palatal – the tooth surface that is situated on the upper teeth that faces the palate.

Lingual – the tooth surface that faces the tongue side of the lower teeth.

Labial – the surface used to describe the outer surface of the anterior (canine, lateral and central) teeth.

Posterior – the surface used to describe the outer surface of the back premolar and molar teeth.

There are 20 deciduous teeth and 32 permanent teeth. Occasionally teeth are congenitally missing or supernumerary teeth may be present (which is when an excess number of teeth are present, more than the normal number). The commonest teeth that can be missing are the second permanent molars, third permanent molars and upper lateral incisors. Less commonly missing teeth are the canines. Congenital absence of teeth is called anodontia. If several teeth, but not all, are congenitally missing the condition is called hypodontia.

Teeth can also have unusual forms. These are listed below:

- Peg laterals – rotated or peg-shaped upper lateral teeth (tooth).
- Turner's tooth – part of the enamel is discoloured and malformed.
- Dentinogenesis imperfecta – when the dentine is malformed on several teeth, and the teeth do not generally grow properly above the gum level.
- Hutchinson's incisors – incisors on which the enamel has deep central grooves.
- Dental fluorosis – where the teeth are mottled due to an excessive intake of fluoride when the teeth were calcifying.
- Enamel hypoplasia – the enamel does not form properly and makes the tooth/teeth less resistant to decay.
- Amelogenesis imperfecta – where the ameloblasts do not lay down the enamel properly, causing irregular demineralisation, presenting as an 'orange peel' effect on the enamel surface.
- Dens in dente – where there is a congenital 'fold' into the tooth enamel (usually in the lateral incisor), causing the tooth to appear conical in shape.
- Taurodontism – where the molar tooth is elongated and has an enlarged, rectangular, coronal pulp chamber.
- Dilaceration – where the root of the tooth is severely angulated/bent.
- Fusion/gemination – where there appears to be a 'double' tooth, due to malformation of the tooth germ. This can be bilateral.
- Cusp of Carabelli – often seen on the upper first molar, this extra cusp lies on the mesiopalatal surface.

Morphology of the dentition

Tables 2.2 and 2.3 give the number of roots and cusps on deciduous and permanent teeth. The shaded areas in the tables represent the teeth.

The are several differences between deciduous and permanent teeth. Deciduous teeth are whiter than permanent teeth, and have more bulbous crowns. The roots of deciduous teeth are more splayed. This is nature's way of allowing space for the developing crowns of the permanent teeth, which are under the roots of the deciduous teeth. The apices of the roots of deciduous teeth are wider than in the permanent teeth. This is of benefit because should an infection occur, drainage is easier, ie an infected deciduous tooth can self-drain through a sinus (gumboil). However, in permanent teeth, an apical abscess, which forms when there is infection, causes extreme pressure on the narrow apex of a permanent tooth. The enamel on deciduous teeth is thinner, and the pulp chambers in deciduous teeth are larger. The latter unfortunately increases the rate of any decay, which reaches the pulp a lot quicker. Deciduous teeth are smaller than permanent teeth, as are the jaws in which they form.

Table 2.2 Number of roots and cusps in deciduous teeth

ROOTS

2	2	1	1	1	1	1	1	2	2
E	D	C	B	A	A	B	C	D	E
E	D	C	B	A	A	B	C	D	E
2	2	1	1	1	1	1	1	2	2

CUSPS

2	2	1	1	1	1	1	1	2	2
E	D	C	B	A	A	B	C	D	E
E	D	C	B	A	A	B	C	D	E
2	2	1	1	1	1	1	1	2	2

Table 2.3 Number of roots and cusps in permanent teeth

ROOTS

3	3	3	1	2	1	1	1	1	1	1	2	1	3	3	3
8	7	6	5	4	3	2	1	1	2	3	4	5	6	7	8
8	7	6	5	4	3	2	1	1	2	3	4	5	6	7	8
2	2	2	1	1	1	1	1	1	1	1	1	1	2	2	2

CUSPS

4	4	4	2	2	1	1	1	1	1	1	2	2	4	4	4
8	7	6	5	4	3	2	1	1	2	3	4	5	6	7	8
8	7	6	5	4	3	2	1	1	2	3	4	5	6	7	8
4	4	5	4	2	1	1	1	1	1	1	2	4	5	4	4

3 Health and Safety

3: Health and Safety

Before starting work, you should be aware of the precautions to take with regard to your own health and safety. Your should protect yourself by being up to date with immunisations. All childhood immunisations should have been carried out, as well as protection against the risks of hepatitis B. Eye tests should also be up to date. *Some* employers (usually health authorities) pay for eye tests and contribute towards the cost of spectacles and contact lenses.

Personal protective equipment (PPE) should be worn by all staff and patients to minimise the risk of transmitting any viruses and bacteria. You will be working in close proximity to your patients and using machinery, such as air rota handpieces and ultrasonic tips, that spray water into patients' mouths, which can then spray onto your clothing. PPE includes a protective bib and goggles for your patient, and masks and gloves for both yourself and the dentist/hygienist.

The Health and Safety at Work Act 1974 states that all employers should take reasonable care of their employees' health and safety, and cooperate fully with them so that they can carry out their tasks safely. Health and safety rules should be prominently displayed, and all employees should let you know of their whereabouts. Your employers also have to comply strictly with these rules, or face disciplinary procedures, a heavy fine or, at worst, imprisonment.

Any machinery that you are expected to use should be demonstrated to you, so that you are aware of any risks, how to use the machinery properly, and how and when to service it. Health and safety covers all rooms in your workplace and even the kitchen should have safety rules displayed on the notice boards.

Any heavy objects that you are manually expected to lift should be carefully judged, so that the weight is manageable, and, if not, that sufficient assistance is available to help you. You should also check that the space that you will be transporting the object(s) within is not obstructed and carries no risks, such as loose rugs, frayed carpets or other obstructing objects on the floor, such as children's toys and magazines. You should also be aware of the path that you are going to take, such as stairs or rise/fall in the flooring. It is important to ensure that the building is clean and tidy at all times, so that others are protected from possible accidents.

Accident reporting

Accidents should always be recorded in the accident report book. The legislation that this falls under is called 'Reporting of Injuries Diseases and Dangerous Occurrences Regulations 1995' (RIDDOR), which is explained later in this chapter. You will need to include the following information:

- Date and time of the accident
- Name of the injured person
- Location of the accident
- The nature of the injury
- The circumstances leading up to the accident
- Anybody else involved
- Type of first aid given.

Other incidents that should be recorded

Violence and aggression should not be tolerated in any shape or form. If you are conscious that this is imminent, you should be aware of how to protect yourself and others, with minimum intervention and maximum safety. Wherever possible, try to alert other staff members and try to diffuse the situation by being as calm as possible. You will not fail by having to leave the scene when an aggressive person is present. Always write every single incident down in an incident book (no matter how minor) and, if the aggressive person is a patient, on their patient record card.

In the event of other colleagues being offensive or bullying in any way, this should always be reported and never tolerated. Disciplinary action should always be put in place. A useful website for guidance regarding this problem is www.workplacebullying.co.uk.

Safety with equipment and machinery

The equipment that you may come into contact with in the dental surgery will probably be: the autoclave, ultrasonic machine, dental chair, amalgam mixers, handpieces and X-ray machinery. It is important to be aware of legislation regarding any machinery, in order to maintain quality and safety and to organise repair should anything at all go wrong. Machinery that is associated with hazardous substances, such as amalgam mixers and X-ray machinery, needs particular care and attention. If the legislation is not followed it could result in dire consequences.

Hazardous waste should be disposed of carefully. This includes sharps, containers of which should be filled no more than two-thirds full. Infectious material should be disposed of in clinical waste sacks. Compressed gases and chemicals such as etchants and bonding materials, which are also hazardous, should be disposed of following the manufacturer's instructions correctly.

PROMOTING STANDARDS OF HEALTH AND SAFETY IN THE WORKPLACE

Below are some of the ways in which you can promote high standards of health and safety in the workplace:

- Your employer's health and safety poster will need to be displayed, or you will need to have a copy of the same inform- ation from your employer. Any workplace where there are five or more employees must have a written health and safety policy.

- Any previous injuries and incidents need to be logged in the accident report book – this will assist in the prevention of any new incidents/accidents from the same cause.

- Be aware of the meaning of the words 'hazard' and 'risk'. Hazard means anything that can cause potential harm. Risk refers to the potential danger from the hazard that can occur, however low or high.

- Be able to perform a 'risk assessment'. This is when a full assessment of the workplace (or other) is carried out for any potential hazards. This is the law, and all employers where there are five or more staff need to be able to perform an adequate and regular risk assessment, and report any health and safety issues.

- Your employer needs to provide health and safety training for you and your colleagues.

How to write a risk assessment

There are five stages to work through to write a risk assessment:

1 Walk around your workplace and look for hazards that could result in harm to others. These could be frayed carpets, loose/damaged electrical wiring, obstruction on the floor, etc. Inform your employer.

2 Decide who may be harmed and how? This may also cover patients, who may not even be present in the building at the time.

3 Take sufficient action to reduce/remove the risk.

4 Record your findings/actions.

5 Do regular reviews of your assessment, and inform others of your actions. This must be done in collaboration with your employer.

Factors to consider when writing a risk assessment:

- Slips, trips and falls
- Lifting heavy objects/manual handling
- Correct disposal of sharps
- Use X-ray machinery and solutions
- Use of anaesthetic and sedation medicaments, and other gases
- Working conditions too hot/too cold/too damp

COSHH and RIDDOR: 'What do they mean, and how do they affect me and my colleagues?'

COSHH

COSSH is the acronym for Control of Substances Hazardous to Health regulations 1999. These regulations are designed to protect employees against any recognised hazards, eg needle-stick injuries, and exposure to chemicals (such as mercury, acid etchant, developing solutions) and electrical equipment. Risk assessment is an invaluable part of controlling such hazards, as identification is the first part of prevention. Hazardous waste should be collected and stored correctly and safely, and placed in the correct containers before collection to avoid unnecessary accidents. These include sharps bins, clinical waste and special waste.

Regular assessments should be carried out for all hazardous equipment, and risk assessment reports should be kept on the premises for others to access. If a risk is present or is likely, then the following steps should be taken:

1 Remove the substance/item from use.

2 Change the working practice, with agreement from your employer, and inform others of the change.

3 Use a less hazardous substance/technique/approach.

4 Review and monitor the changes regularly.

RIDDOR 1995

Any accidents and diseases that are brought into or occur in the workplace should be logged and reported under this legislation. For example:

- Needle-stick injuries

- Transfer of blood-borne diseases (eg hepatitis, HIV)

- Injury that results in the worker being off work for three days or longer

- If an employee is killed or taken to hospital as a result of an accident at work, then the Health and Safety Executive needs to be informed. This then has to be followed up by the writing of a completed accident report form (F2508).

FIRE SAFETY

Fire safety is an ongoing awareness for all members of staff in the workplace. This should be integrated as part of regular staff training, and should be logged detailing all the staff who attended, the dates and the nature of the training given, as well as who instructed the fire precautions.

FIRE SAFETY TRAINING SHOULD INCLUDE:

- Actions to be taken when discovering a fire
- Actions that are taken upon hearing the fire alarm
- Operating the fire alarm
- Calling the fire brigade
- How to use fire-fighting equipment
- Purpose of fire-resisting doors
- Familiarity with all fire escape routes, which should be clearly marked
- Evacuation and all assembly points.

A fire marshall should be allocated to each floor of the premises. Their responsibilities should include the implementation and co-ordination of the action taken in case of a fire. Fire drills should also be taken into account with disabled people, and their means of escape, as this can differ according to their disability. It must be remembered that lifts should not be used unless the fire authority have advised and authorised this.

FIRE-FIGHTING EQUIPMENT

Fire fighting equipment should be easily accessible, and examined on an annual basis in accordance with British Standards, by a qualified and competent person. Once tested, the date of the test should be clearly marked. All hose reels should also be tested on an annual basis, and recorded in the log book.

There are different types of fire extinguishers. All are coloured red, with a single colour identification band around the top of the cylinder:

- **RED** = Water – used for paper, textile and solid material fires – NOT TO BE USED ON LIQUID, ELECTRICAL or METAL FIRES.
- **BLUE** = Powder – for liquid and electrical fires – NOT TO BE USED ON METAL FIRES.
- **CREAM** = Foam – to be used on liquid fires. NOT TO BE USED ON ELECTRICAL OR METAL FIRES.
- **BLACK** = Carbon Dioxide – for liquid and electrical fires – NOT TO BE USED ON METAL FIRES.

These extinguishers were brought in line with European standards on 15 May 1996 under BS EN3 1996, which allowed fire extinguishers to be only red in colour, although allowing up to 5% of the external area to be a different colour in order to identify the type of substance inside.

Services are advised to keep all fire-fighting equipment in good working order.

Standard service

- A service agreement that will **include all minor spare parts**, but exclude discharge tests, refills, major spares and hydraulic stretch tests.

- Hose reels can be included within the standard service.

Comprehensive service

- This service **includes all minor spares, discharge tests and refills** but excludes major spares and hydraulic stretch tests.

- Hose reels can also be included. These service contracts include a detailed report following a visit.

Safety with electrical sockets

- It is important not to use several electrical adaptors. This will cause an overload within the circuitry and cause the wiring to overheat and start a fire. Only one device per outlet is advised in order to prevent this.

Fire blankets: for fires involving both solids and liquids.

- Good for small fires in clothing and for chip and fat pan fires, provided that the blanket completely covers the fire. Protect yourself and turn off the heat source.

- Can be used to smother a fire on a person's clothing. The fire blanket needs to cover the entire fire on the person or it may not work effectively.

- Place the blanket carefully over the fire. Keep your hands shielded from the fire.

Useful websites with health & safety information:

- www.hse.gov.uk – the Health and Safety Executive: which is responsible for the regulation of almost all the risks to health and safety arising from work activity in Britain.

- www.odpm.gov.uk – the Office of the Deputy Prime Minister, which is responsible for policy on housing, planning, regional and local government and the fire service.

- www.bsi-global.com – the British Standards Institute; contains information regarding national and international standards. They also supply advice on what key standards apply to businesses in various sectors.

Action in the event of a fire

The fire alarm should be set off, 999 dialled, fire service requested and the building evacuated. If possible, the day book/diary should be taken, so that everyone in the building can be accounted for. Fire extinguishers should always be kept in an accessible place and in good working order, plus a fire blanket. All staff should know where they are and how to use them. A fire evacuation procedure should be in place and regularly practised with all members of staff. There should be clearly marked guidance as to where the nearest fire exit is, as well as the nearest gathering point, so that evacuation can be done quickly and efficiently. Practice of fire evacuation procedures is essential.

Lighting, heating and ventilation

You should avoid reflection of natural light, that is glare from a VDU screen. Anti-glare screens can be fitted. Light flickering from these should be reported. VDUs should not be operated for more than two hours at a time without a break. There should be correctly fitted artificial lights, with the correct quantity of light units to avoid eye strain. Adequate ventilation should be present to avoid inhalation of accumulated fumes, overheating and to promote cross infection control and general comfort. Equipment such as autoclaves and office equipment all generate additional heat and should be taken into consideration when placing and using them.

Noise control

Distraction from outside noise and/or adjacent surgeries is difficult to avoid, but careful positioning of reception areas, and items such as sound-proofed printer covers, can be of assistance.

Moving and handling

When lifting heavy and/or bulky objects, a risk assessment can be done to see whether or not the item can be safely moved. Wherever possible, keep objects close to you. Carry objects with others to divide the weight. Make sure that objects, such as boxes of stock deliveries, are not in the way of others.

KEY TERMS	
COSHH	Control of Substances Hazardous to Health
RIDDOR	Reporting of Injuries, Diseases and Dangerous Occurrences Regulations
Health and Safety Executive	This is responsible for the regulation of almost all the risks to health and safety arising from work activities in Britain, and must be informed in the event of major problems in the workplace, such as a large mercury spillage
Blood-borne diseases	Diseases that are transmitted through the blood of the carrier
PPE	Personal protective equipment is the equipment that is used to protect against the spread of infection, such as gloves, goggles, masks, protective aprons.

Medical emergencies in the dental surgery

A medical emergency can occur in the dental surgery at any time. The casualty could be a patient, someone accompanying a patient, a visitor to the practice or another member of staff. It is therefore important to realise that an emergency may not necessarily occur as a direct result of the person's medical history, but can also be as a result of an

JET LIBRARY

accident that has taken place on the surgery premises. Hence it is essential that dental nurses are confident and capable of fulfilling their role in the event of such an emergency. Dentists need to ensure that all members of the dental team are properly trained and prepared.

The General Dental Council requires all dental practices to practise resuscitation routines at regular intervals. Each practice should also have a range of equipment and drugs available on the premises. Emergency equipment should be stored in the correct designated area of the practice, and everyone should be aware of its location should it be required. Equipment should always be returned to its correct place after use. Labels should be used to show where equipment is stored.

All emergency equipment should be regularly checked and serviced as requested by the manufacturer. A full record, displaying service and maintenance, should also be kept. Any faults in equipment must be reported immediately and repairs or replacement of equipment carried out.

It is recommended that all dental practices should have the following equipment available:

- Portable oxygen, mask, tubing
- Suction equipment
- Bag, valve and mask with reservoir
- Nasal airways
- Oropharyngeal airways
- Hand-operated suction.

Emergency drugs (Fig. 3.1) held on the surgery premises should, as with equipment, be stored in designated areas of the practice. They should be readily available during the times when the practice is operational, but should be locked away at the end of each working day or at times when the surgery is not open. All staff should be made aware of the location of emergency drugs, but they should be handled or administered only by suitably qualified, designated members of the dental team. An up-to-date inventory should be kept of all drugs and supplies should be regularly checked for shelf-life so that they do not go out of date. Drugs used should immediately be replenished to ensure that a full range is available if the need arises.

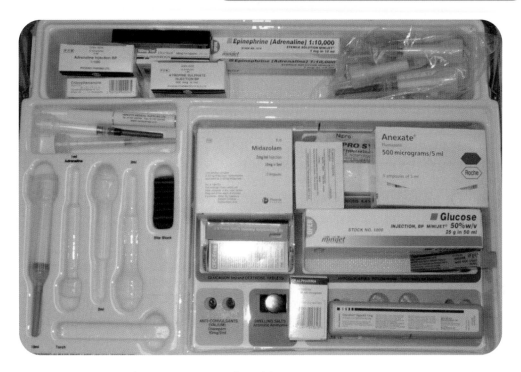

Fig. 3.1 Contents of an emergency drug kit.

It is recommended that the following drugs be held within each dental practice:

- Glucose powder
- Glucagon injection (1 unit vial with solvent)
- Intravenous glucose infusion 50% (1 x 50 ml pre-filled syringe)
- Hydrocortisone injection (100 mg vial and 2 ml sterile water for injection)
- Glyceryl trinitrate sprays and tablets
- Diazepam injection (5 mg/ml, 3 x 2 ml ampoule)
- Chlorphenamine injection (10 mg/ml, 3 x 1 ml ampoule)
- Adrenaline (epinephrine) 1:1000
- Salbutamol inhaler
- Salbutamol for intravenous injection (500 micrograms/ml – 1 ml ampoule)
- Aspirin tablets (300 mg).

Although emergency equipment and drugs are readily available to treat any emergency incidents that may arise in the dental surgery, it is often the dental team's first intervention that is of paramount importance when responding to a medical emergency.

Being able to distinguish signs and listening to symptoms of a casualty is of utmost importance in recognising and treating successfully medical emergencies that may occur. You should be able to assess each situation, and thus always ensure that in treating each emergency you do not put yourself at risk — this should always be a priority. Other important factors to be considered include ensuring that you follow the procedure of your workplace when dealing with an emergency, and, if you are doubtful of what to do in a situation, being able to summon others for help.

To enable dental nurses to have the confidence and experience to deal with a medical emergency, they need to be appropriately educated and adequately trained. In this chapter we identify a range of emergencies that could occur in the dental practice. We will look at signs and symptoms that enable the dental nurse to identify the condition correctly and then act accordingly. As already stated above, the first rule of giving first aid is at all times to maintain your own safety. Try to stay calm at all times, even when the situation that you are dealing with may be alarming. Where possible, try to enlist the help of another responsible person who could be used if required to summon help, call an ambulance, help control bleeding or observe the casualty.

Accidents and injuries

Accidents and resulting injuries can happen in any area of the dental practice. They can occur as a result of a slip, trip or fall either inside or outside the practice, or as a result of a burn or electrocution in the kitchen area or surgery. Objects in the eye, cuts and grazes, or more serious wounds can also occur as a result of accidents that happen in the workplace.

THE DENTAL NURSE'S RESPONSIBILITIES IN FIRST AID

- To assess the situation safely and quickly, and summon appropriate help.

- To identify as far as possible the injury, or nature of the illness affecting the casualty.

- To give early, appropriate and adequate treatment in a sensible order of priority.

- To summon assistance straight away.

- To remain with the casualty until appropriate help arrives.

- To arrange for removal of the casualty to hospital if appropriate.

- To pass on accurate information detailing the event as it happened and any assistance given. Medical emergencies can occur either in the dental surgery or in other areas on the premises. They can occur as a direct result of an accident or injury, an ongoing health condition or the onset of a medical condition.

Eye injuries

The commonest eye injury is a result of small particles of dust or debris entering the eye. To prevent such an injury happening at the chairside, all dental staff should be encouraged to wear eye protection at all times while treating patients and assisting during dental procedures.

Treatment

- Encourage the casualty not to rub the injured eye, as this may further damage the eye.

- Ask the patient to sit down, if standing, and reassure them.

- Gently examine the injured eye thoroughly to locate the foreign body.

- If the foreign body is visible on the white area of the eye, try to remove it by using a sterile eyewash, asking the casualty to tip or tilt the head to the side and running the solution from the inside of the eye out, so that the object is washed from the eye and not dislodged further into the eye and socket.

- A clean tissue or damp sterile swab may also be used if the eyewash is unsuccessful.

- If the object cannot be removed then further medical assistance will be necessary.

- Report the injury in the practice accident book.

Burns

A burn is damage to the skin caused by extremes of temperatures, eg:

- Heat (dry burn) – flame from a Bunsen burner/handling an instrument that has been held in the flame of a Bunsen burner.

- Chemical – corrosive substances such as bleach/acid etch.

- Scald (wet burn) – steam from an autoclave or kettle/hot liquids.

- Cold burns – ethyl chloride.

- Electrical – faulty plugs or fuses/electrical surgery or kitchen equipment.

The treatment of burns can vary depending on the type of burn suffered by the casualty, but in all cases the treatment should commence straight away. The first stage of treatment requires the type and extent of burn to be assessed.

Minor burns

- Immediately cool the affected area by placing the injury under cool running water for at least 10 minutes.

- Remove any jewellery likely to cause constriction before the swelling occurs.

- Cover the area with a clean and sterile dressing.

- Never puncture any blisters that may form on the burn.

- Report in the accident book.

Severe burns

When dealing with severe burns there are two major factors to consider – shock (caused by loss of fluids from the burn) and infection (extremely high risk).

- Reassure the casualty and help them lie down.

- Do not remove any clothing from the burn site as this may cause further tissue damage, because an item of clothing may have stuck to the surface of the skin.

- Dial 999 straight away to request an ambulance.

- Cool the affected area with water for at least 20 minutes.

- Remove any jewellery that may become constrictive if swelling occurs.

- Cover the burn site with a clean and sterile dressing. If the burn site is too large for a dressing then cover with Clingfilm or a clean plastic bag to minimise the risk of infection.

- Monitor and reassure the casualty until the ambulance arrives.

- Report in the accident book.

Chemical burns

- Wear protective gloves, apron and glasses.

- Douse the affected area with water for 20 minutes.

- Dress the burn with a sterile dressing.

- Seek medical assistance – transfer to hospital.

- Ensure that any chemical waste is disposed of correctly.

- Report in the accident book.

Electrocution

Electrocution is caused by the passage of an electrical current through the body, resulting in burns and interference with the heart beat, by making it beat erratically or stopping it completely. Electrocution could happen in any area of the surgery as a result of faulty equipment or electrical sockets, plugs and wires.

Treatment

- Assess the situation. Never approach or touch the casualty without switching off the source of electricity. If you are in any doubt do not touch the casualty and get help straight away.

- If able to switch off current do so.
- Assess the casualty. Are they breathing? Have they got a pulse?
- Summon help straight away: dial 999.
- Commence cardiopulmonary resuscitation (CPR) if casualty is not breathing and no pulse can be found.
- If patient is breathing, cover any burns with sterile dressing.
- Monitor casualty carefully until ambulance arrives.

Dealing with wounds

Types of wounds

Incised – Clean cut from a sharp edge such as a blade or broken glass.

Laceration – A rough tear.

Abrasion – A graze in which the top layer of skin is scraped off, leaving a raw tender area.

Contusion – A bruise.

Puncture wound – Small site of entry, but can cause a deep track of internal damage.

Wounds can occur in the dental surgery as a result of various accidents and injuries. It is extremely important that all wounds are correctly treated straight away to limit the risk of infection and cross-infection.

Treatment

- Wear gloves and wash the wound under running water.
- Gently dry the wound with a swab.
- Cover with a sterile dressing of a suitable size.
- Report in the accident book.

Bleeding wounds

In serious or extensive wounds that involve major blood vessels uncontrolled blood loss can occur. In such cases, it is essential that the loss of blood should be controlled as soon as possible to prevent the casualty suffering from shock.

Treatment

- Always wear gloves.
- Reassure the casualty. Ensure that they are lying down and warm.
- Apply direct pressure onto the wound using a clean dressing.
- Elevate the injured limb.
- Secure the wound dressing with a bandage that is tight enough to maintain pressure on the wound.
- If the wound continues to bleed through the dressing and bandage, place a second dressing and bandage on top of the original.
- If bleeding still persists remove both dressings and bandages, and place fresh bandages and dressings, ensuring that the pressure point is accurate with regard to the area that is bleeding.
- Support the injured limb, ensuring that it remains elevated.
- Dial 999 for transfer to hospital via ambulance.

Object in wound

- Never remove an object from a wound as this could make the injury worse.
- When applying pressure to this type of wound do not press the object into the wound. Apply pressure around the edges of the wound instead.
- If placing a dressing on the injury roll up two sterile dressings, placing one on either side of the wound and object. Hold the dressings in place with a clean bandage, again ensuring that it does not interfere with the object.
- Support and elevate the limb.
- Dial 999 for transfer to hospital via ambulance.
- Monitor and reassure the casualty.

Fractures

A fracture is a broken bone. It can be a crack in the bone or a clean break or shattering of bone (as in a crush injury). A fractured bone can remain under intact skin; this is known as a closed fracture. If the fractured bone has come through the skin this is known as an open fracture. This type of fracture can involve loss of blood and a greater chance of infection. A complicated fracture is where there is additional damage to a nearby organ or tissues, eg lung damage from a fractured rib.

The signs of a fracture include:

- deformity
- pain
- swelling
- wound with bone end penetrating.

THE DENTAL NURSE'S ROLE IN THE TREATMENT OF FRACTURES

- Ensure that the casualty is not given anything to eat or drink (in case they need to be given a general anaesthetic).

- Treat the casualty where they are – do not move them unless they are in immediate danger.

- Make sure the casualty keeps still.

- In the case of open fractures, dress the wound and apply pressure to stem the flow of blood around the bone before immobilising the injured area. Do not attempt to straighten the injured limb. To immobilise the injured area, bandage it to an unaffected area of the body, eg support an injured leg by bandaging it to the uninjured leg.

- Ensure that arrangements are made to transport the patient to hospital.

- Monitor the casualty and if necessary treat the patient for shock.

- Do not move the patient until the injured area is fully secured and supported.

The first aid box

All dental practices should hold a fully stocked first aid box. The following items are recommended:

- First aid guidance notes
- Individually wrapped sterile adhesive dressings
- Medium sterile dressings
- Large sterile dressings
- Triangular bandages, individually wrapped and preferably sterile
- Sterile eye pads with attachments
- Safety pins
- Crepe roller bandages
- Non-alcoholic wound-cleansing wipes
- Sterile eye wash solution
- Scissors
- Cotton wool
- Adhesive tape
- Disposable gloves
- Disposable plastic aprons.

All staff should be aware of where the first aid box is located. It is essential that the stock in the first aid box be controlled and maintained, and that expiry dates on the contents of the first aid box are also monitored. If unused items are past their expiry date they should be disposed of and replaced. Used items need to be replaced in the first aid box to ensure that the stock is always maintained.

Dressings and bandages

Dressings

Dressings are used to control bleeding and protect the wound from getting infected. Wherever possible sterile dressings should always be used. Rules for applying dressings are as follows:

- Dressings should be large enough to extend beyond the edges of the wound.
- Dressings should be placed directly onto the wound – do not move them about.
- If blood seeps through the dressing, apply another one over it.

Bandages

Bandages are used to:

- maintain direct pressure over a dressing
- hold dressings and splints in place
- limit swelling
- provide support to a limb or joint
- restrict movement.

There are three main types of bandage: triangular, roller and tubular.

Triangular bandages are usually made from strung cotton that does not stretch. They can be used for a number of purposes:

- Improvised dressing pads
- Folded broadly to support and immobilise limbs, secure splints and bulky dressings
- Folded narrowly to provide a bandage that secures dressings to limbs
- Opened and shaped to provide a dressing for hand, foot or scalp wounds
- As slings.

Roller bandages are used to secure dressings and give support to injured limbs.

Tubular bandages are used to secure dressings and give support to injured limbs.

GENERAL RULES FOR APPLYING BANDAGES

- Work in front of the casualty and from the injured side wherever possible.

- Explain to the casualty what you are doing, reassure them and enlist their help wherever possible.

- Keep injured part supported.

- Apply bandages firmly enough to control bleeding and hold a dressing securely in place but not too tight so as not to impair circulation.

- Leave fingers and toes exposed if possible to check circulation.

- If tying a bandage, use a reef knot as they lie flat, do not slip and are quickly released.

It is necessary that once you have bandaged a limb the circulation be checked every 10 minutes, as swelling can occur after injury. Signs of impaired circulation include:

- pale, cold skin on hands or feet
- dusky grey or blue appearance on the skin
- patient complaining of tingling or numbness.

To check the circulation press on one of the nails or skin of the hand/foot until it becomes pale. On releasing, the colour should quickly return; if it does not the bandage is too tight.

Medical emergencies

Making a diagnosis

To enable the dental nurse to be able to act quickly and correctly, and to follow the correct procedures when handling a medical emergency, a diagnosis must be made to establish the patient's condition. A diagnosis is made by a careful examination using three types of clue.

History – This is information given by the casualty him- or herself, or by witnesses. Check if there is already any information in the patient notes regarding any past or present medical conditions. Is the patient taking medication?

Signs – These are clues that you find using your own resources when examining the casualty, eg:

- How the patient looks – pale/flushed
- How the patient feels – hot/cold/clammy
- How the patient sounds – coherent/confused
- Any evidence of bleeding/vomit/urine.

Symptoms – These are sensations felt by the casualty, such as cold, nausea, heat, pain, dizziness, and about which they inform you.

Conditions when a casualty can become unconscious

Unconsciousness is defined as an interruption in the normal activity of the brain.

Fainting

A faint is caused by a temporary reduction in the flow of blood to the brain. Unlike shock, the pulse becomes very slow but usually picks up quickly, and recovery is rapid and complete. A patient who is in pain, emotionally upset or frightened of visiting the dental practice can faint. Exhaustion and lack of food are also reasons why a patient may faint. A faint should last only a short period of time, and is followed by an improvement in blood flow to the brain.

Symptoms of fainting – The patient may complain of feeling hot, dizzy and sick.

Signs of fainting – The patient will appear to become very pale, with the skin feeling cold and clammy. They may appear unsteady on their feet if they are standing.

If the patient is conscious the treatment is as follows:

- Lay the casualty down and raise the legs above the level of the head.
- Loosen any tight clothing.

- Open the windows, and switch on the fan to ventilate and cool the immediate area.

- As the patient begins to recover offer them a glucose drink (as long as there are no medical contraindications).

- When they have fully recovered help the casualty to sit up slowly.

If the patient is unconscious the treatment is as follows:

- Ensure that the patient's airway is maintained.

- Raise the legs above the level of the head.

- Loosen any tight clothing.

- Open the windows, and switch on the fan to ventilate the immediate area.

- Stay with the casualty and monitor them until they fully recover consciousness.

- Reassure the patient when they recover.

- Offer a glucose drink (if there are no medical contraindications).

- After the patient has fully recovered help them to sit up slowly.

Principles of resuscitation (basic life support)

The purpose of CPR is to try to maintain the same level of oxygenation in the brain and other vital organs of the body until the arrival of the emergency services. A **respiratory arrest** is an accident such as drowning, smoke inhalation or choking that stops breathing for up to two minutes, but the heart keeps beating. A **cardiac arrest** means that something has caused the heart to stop beating, with breathing also stopping. Examples include a heart attack or electrocution.

It is essential that in both cases action should be taken immediately. All dental practice staff should routinely take part in CPR training to ensure that they can all act quickly and correctly in the event of a collapse in the dental surgery. It is important that all members of staff fully understand and can follow practice procedures when dealing with a casualty who requires CPR or basic life support.

The three elements of basic life support

Airway (A)

To maintain a clear airway keep the casualty's head back by lifting the chin. In this tilted position the tongue is lifted away from the back of the throat so that it does not block the trachea.

Breathing (B)

Establish whether or not the casualty is breathing. By placing your ear close to the casualty's mouth you can hear breathing, feel their breath on the side of your face, and watch the chest move up and down. If a casualty is not breathing then you can give mouth-to-mouth resuscitation.

Circulation (C)

If you have been trained to check the carotid pulse, you may do so for up to 10 seconds. If not, assess the circulation by looking for signs of life. If there are no signs and you believe that the heart has stopped you must begin chest compressions combined with mouth-to-mouth resuscitation.

Assessment of the casualty

- Check whether the casualty is responsive. Gently shake them, say their name, ask if they are okay.

- If the patient responds to you by answering or nodding/moving, reassure them. Check for any injuries and then go for help.

- If the casualty does not respond to your voice – shout for help, open the airway by tilting the head and lifting the chin, remove any obstructions from the mouth, loosen any restrictive or tight clothing carefully and try not to move the casualty.

- Assessing for breathing – look for chest movement/listen for breathing sounds/feel for air by placing your cheek close to the casualty's mouth. If breathing is present put casualty in the recovery position (see next section).

If the casualty is not breathing

- If there are no signs of breathing get help straight away, either from 999 yourself or sending someone else to ring 999 on your behalf. If you are sending someone else make sure that the person returns once they have made the call to inform you that the ambulance is on the way, and if possible to assist you further until the emergency service arrives.

- Once help has been sought, return to the casualty. Ensure that the airway is maintained by tilting the head and lifting the chin.

- Pinch the soft part of the casualty's nose, ensuring that air cannot escape the nostrils.

- Slightly open the mouth of the casualty.

- Take a breath, place your lips around the patient's mouth to form a seal.

- Breathe steadily into the mouth.

- Observe to see if the casualty's chest rises. The chest should rise; if it does not it may be because the airway is not fully open, an obstruction remains, or the seal around the mouth was not adequate – check again.

- Remove your mouth from the patient's, but maintain an open airway by keeping the head tilted back and the chin lifted.

- Allow the chest to fall as air comes out.

- Take another breath and repeat sequence as before.

- Check for signs of circulation – check for carotid pulse/if you are confident that there are signs of circulation then continue mouth-to-mouth resuscitation until the patient begins to breathe for themselves or until the ambulance arrives.

- Once the patient begins to breathe, place the patient in the recovery position and monitor, checking their pulse and breathing – do not leave the patient.

If the casualty's circulation has stopped

- If you cannot find signs of circulation begin chest compressions straight away.

- Kneel to the side of the patient. Place the heel of one hand two fingers' width above where the casualty's ribs meet their breastbone. Place the other hand on top and interlock the fingers of both hands.

- Lean well over the patient, with arms straight and press down vertically on the sternum to depress it into the chest cavity (approximately 4 cm).

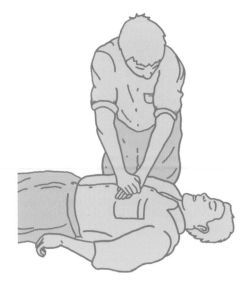

- Release the pressure on the chest, then repeat the action at a rate of 100 chest compressions per minute.
- After 15 compressions, tilt the patient's head and lift the chin, giving the patient two inflations again ensuring that a good seal is made with the lips over the patient's mouth.
- Then give a further 15 chest compressions.
- Continue to give 15 chest compressions to two inflations.

You will need to continue ventilation and chest compressions until the emergency services arrive. If two first-aiders are present they should take it in turns to resuscitate the patient, but each person should complete a cycle before changing over.

The recovery position

- Remove the patient's glasses and keys/bulky items from pockets.
- Kneel beside the patient and position both of the patient's legs so that they are straight.
- By tilting the patient's head back and lifting the chin the airway will be opened.
- Place the arm of the patient that is nearest to you at a right angle to their body, and the elbow bent with the hand uppermost.

- Bring the arm away from you across the chest and hold the back of the hand against the cheek.

- Using your other hand, grasp the far leg just below the knee and pull it up, making sure that the foot is on the ground.
- While keeping the patient's hand pressed up against their cheek, pull on the bent leg and roll the patient towards you, onto their side.

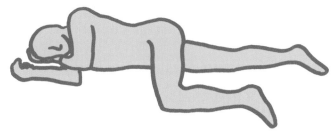

- Adjust the upper leg so that both the hip and the knee are bent at right angles.
- Tilt the head back to ensure that the airway is maintained.
- Adjust the hand under the head to keep the head tilted back.
- Check breathing and circulation.

Shock

The function of the circulatory system is to distribute blood to all parts of the body so that oxygen and nutrients within the blood can be absorbed into the tissues of the body. Shock causes a lack of circulatory fluid as a result of some breakdown in the circulatory system. Causes of shock can vary from heart attack, burns and scalds to wounds where a quantity of blood is lost or fractures.

The body responds to shock by withdrawing the blood supply from the surface to the care of the body's vital organs. Shock can be worsened when the patient is in pain or frightened. Most adults can afford to lose a pint of blood without any ill-effect, but if bleeding continues the body begins to shut down. Adrenaline (epinephrine) is released into the bloodstream causing a rapid pulse, sweating and cold clammy skin. The skin also becomes pale. As shock continues, the patient begins to feel weak, giddy, sick and thirsty. Their breathing becomes rapid and shallow and they complain of feeling breathless. The patient will slip into unconsciousness and finally their heart will stop.

THE DENTAL NURSE'S ROLE IN THE MANAGEMENT OF SHOCK

- Treat any obvious cause of shock if possible (eg bleeding from a wound).
- Call for an ambulance.
- Lay the patient down, ensuring that the head is kept lower than the feet so that the brain is not deprived of oxygen.
- Raising the legs encourages blood to flow into the vital organs.
- Loosen tight clothing.
- Keep the patient warm with blankets.
- Remain with the patient at all times and constantly reassure them.
- Monitor the patient by checking their levels of response and their pulse at regular intervals.
- Be prepared to resuscitate the patient if necessary.

Heart disorders

Angina pectoris

This term describes the pain experienced by a patient when the coronary arteries are unable to dilate sufficiently to supply the heart with enough oxygen during activity. The patient will experience a gripping pain in the chest, which often radiates down the left arm. The patient will also experience shortness of breath and tingling in the hands.

THE DENTAL NURSE'S ROLE IN THE MANAGEMENT OF A PATIENT WITH ANGINA PECTORIS

- Reassure the patient.

- If they have medication for this condition ensure that they take it, according to their doctor's instructions, assisting them if need be. The medication will ease the pain by causing dilatation of the coronary arteries.

Coronary thrombosis

The pain is the same as that of angina, but much worse. Pain is not eased with rest and the patient may vomit with signs of shock also shown.

THE DENTAL NURSE'S ROLE IN THE MANAGEMENT OF A PATIENT WITH CORONARY THROMBOSIS

- Ring 999 straight away.

- Position the patient in a half-sitting position and support their back.

- Loosen clothing and reassure the patient.

- Be ready to commence CPR if the patient collapses.

Anaphylactic shock

The term describes a massive allergic reaction, which may develop within seconds of exposure to a substance, that is potentially fatal. The substance can be anything from drugs to nuts, insect bites or seafood. The reaction causes massive amounts of a histamine-type substance to be released into the body's tissues. Breathing may become difficult as the trachea swells, blocking the airway. The skin develops weals of blotchy eruptions, and the face becomes swollen and distorted. The casualty is often panic stricken.

Management

- Reassure the patient.

- In mild reactions antihistamine drugs are given.

- In more severe allergic reactions an injection of adrenaline is administered to counteract the poisonous effect of the allergy, and the patient will be admitted to hospital.

Epilepsy

This is a condition where the patient suffers from convulsions (fits). Epilepsy is caused by abnormal electrical activity in the brain. There are three types of epilepsy:

1 Petit mal – lapses of awareness

2 Grand mal – classic, more severe convulsions

3 Status epilepticus – continuous convulsions.

Signs and symptoms

- Patient loses consciousness.

- The body becomes rigid.

- This is followed by uncontrolled jerking movements.

- Patients may sometimes become incontinent.

- Once the convulsions cease, the patient may sleep.

THE DENTAL NURSE'S ROLE IN THE MANAGEMENT OF AN EPILEPTIC ATTACK

- Move any furniture or equipment to prevent the patient from injuring themselves.

- Summon help.

- Maintain the patient's airway.

- Administer oxygen.

- Stay with the patient and monitor them until the convulsions ease and eventually stop.

If the patient suffers from status epilepticus it may be necessary to administer diazepam by iv (intravenous) injection (administered by trained clinical staff).

Diabetes

When the amount of blood sugar falls below a certain level, the brain is rapidly affected. This condition is known as **hypoglycaemia** and is most often found in people who have diabetes. Diabetic patients are usually well aware of their condition and are prepared for an emergency. Provided that the casualty is conscious get them to eat/drink some form of sugar to raise the blood sugar level, either a glucose drink or a sugar-rich food (chocolate/biscuits/cake). A patient experiencing hypoglycaemic attacks will complain of feeling weak; they may also sweat, become aggressive, behave uncharacteristically, become pale, feel faint; and in some cases collapse into unconsciousness. If the patient becomes unconscious it will be impossible to administer sugar orally, and medical intervention is required to administer sugar intravenously.

4 Cross-infection Control and Sterilisation

4: Cross-infection Control and Sterilisation

Before looking at the importance of cross-infection control, we need to understand what we are protecting against. This requires a brief understanding of microbiology.

Microbiology

Micro-organisms, commonly known as germs or microbes, are microscopic living organisms that can cause diseases. Micro-organisms can be transmitted from an infected person to a healthy person, thus spreading an illness or disease. Micro-organisms can be divided into three main groups:

- Bacteria
- Viruses
- Fungi.

Bacteria

Bacteria are single-cell organisms, which are visible when examined with a light microscope. Bacteria are subdivided into groups according to their shape:

- Cocci – these are round in shape (Fig. 4.1a), eg:
    - Streptococci – these grow in single strands (Fig. 4.1b). They cause sore throats and initiate dental decay.
    - Staphylococci – these grow in clumps (Fig. 4.2c). They cause skin boils and gum boils.
- Bacilli – these are rod shaped (Fig. 4.2), eg:
    - Lactobacilli – these are found in decayed teeth.
    - *Bacillus fusiformis* – this is found in cases of acute necrotic ulcerative gingivitis (ANUG).

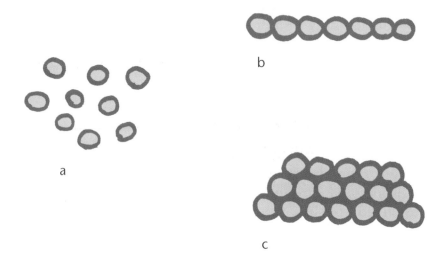

b

a

c

Fig. 4.1 Bacterial shapes: (a) cocci, (b) streptococci, (c) staphylococci.

Fig. 4.2 Bacterial shapes: bacilli.

Spores

Bacterial spores can survive extremes of temperature by forming a hard protective outer shell, which makes them highly resistant. Therefore special methods of sterilisation such as autoclaving are necessary to destroy them.

Viruses

Viruses cannot be seen using an ordinary microscope because they are smaller than bacteria. Most viruses are unaffected by drugs and therefore viral diseases such as acquired immune deficiency syndrome (AIDS) are incurable and fatal. Viruses that cause diseases such as hepatitis B, measles, mumps and rubella can, however, be prevented from multiplying by vaccination. The most effective method of sterilisation to destroy viruses is autoclaving.

Fungi

Under a microscope, fungi appear larger than bacteria. An example of a fungus found in the mouth is *Candida albicans*. This causes denture stomatitis (denture sore mouth, which appears as red areas under dentures or removable orthodontic appliances) and thrush (which appears as white patches on the tongue and other parts of the mouth). Thrush is most commonly found in babies' mouths, or in the mouths of debilitated elderly people. Neither denture stomatitis nor thrush is successfully treated with antibiotics, but can be successfully treated with antifungal agents. Autoclaving can destroy fungal micro-organisms.

What is cross-infection?

Cross-infection in the dental surgery (Fig. 4.3) can be defined as the spread of infection from:

- patient to patient
- patient to dental staff
- dental staff to patient.

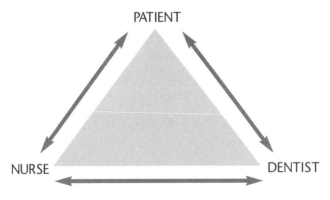

Fig. 4.3 Cross-infection triangle.

Numerous microbes live on the skin, and in the mouth, nose and throat, causing no harm to us because they live on external surfaces. However, they can become harmful if they invade the body's tissues or are transferred from one patient's mouth to another's. In dentistry this can happen if instruments or equipment is not properly sterilised between patients or if surgery hygiene is not maintained. This puts not only other patients at risk but also members of the surgery staff.

When discussing the meaning of cross-infection, it is very important that as members of the dental team we are aware of the occupational hazards related to cross-infection.

Dental procedures often involve the loss of blood. Even the smallest amount of blood can contain viruses, such as the human immunodeficiency virus (HIV), and hepatitis B and C viruses. Cross-infections with these viruses can occur through direct contact with blood on instruments, swabs, etc. Furthermore, they can be sprayed over a wide area of the surgery during the use of ultrasonic scalers, 3-in-1 syringes and handpieces.

Hepatitis B virus

This virus causes the liver to become inflamed. The virus is spread by contact with infected blood. It can be found in all body fluids such as saliva, blood and even breast milk. In some cases a patient who has become infected with the virus and has no symptoms may be unaware that they are carriers of the virus. It is vital that all members of the dental team are vaccinated against this condition before beginning work as a member of the dental profession. The vaccination schedule consists of three separate injections of the vaccine over fixed intervals of time. This is followed by a blood test to ensure that antibodies are present in the blood, thereby protecting the individual from contracting the condition.

HIV and AIDS

HIV attacks the T4 lymphocytes (a type of white blood cell) in the blood by multiplying inside the cells. The cells then die, releasing new virus particles into the blood to infect more cells. A patient suffering from this has a condition called persistent generalised lymphadenopathy, the symptoms of which are fever, weight loss, infections of the mouth and bouts of diarrhoea. In AIDS the white blood cells are destroyed, therefore weakening the body's natural defences, leaving the patient susceptible to infection.

In a dental environment the spread of such illnesses can be prevented by sterilising all instruments, thus preventing the risk of cross-infection.

What is sterilisation?

The process of sterilisation kills all bacteria and fungi, and their spores, and viruses. There are several methods of sterilisation, each of which is suitable for sterilising a range of dental instruments and equipment, and dressings and materials that are used in the dental surgery. All dental equipment comes with specified manufacturers' instructions about the correct method of sterilisation, which must be followed for each item. It is a legal requirement that these instructions are fully followed and adhered to.

Autoclaving

The autoclave works in a similar way to a pressure cooker. Steam is produced inside the autoclave, which reaches a temperature of 134°C for 3 minutes. The autoclave cycle starts from the time when the instruments are placed inside the autoclave and it is switched on. The autoclave cycle includes the time allowed for the heating up to reach the required temperature and the time for the autoclave to cool down before the instruments are removed. The average time for the complete cycle is 20 minutes. It is important to note that instruments should never be removed from the autoclave until the full cycle has been completed. Heat-sensitive items can be autoclaved for 10 minutes at 126°C.

The autoclave method of sterilising is suitable for all metal instruments, rubber equipment, burs, swabs and cotton wool products. Handpieces and orthodontic pliers must be correctly cleaned and lubricated prior to autoclaving. The instruments must be evenly spaced in open containers to make sure that all surfaces of each item are exposed to the autoclave steam.

Vacuum autoclaves

These allow packaged items to be sterilised and to be transferred dry, straight into the storage facility, remaining sterile until the item is used.

How can you be sure that the autoclave is working properly?

Indicator strips that show that the correct temperature has been reached can be placed on the autoclave trays when they are put in the autoclave. Autoclaves need to be regularly serviced, inspected and tested, and a full record of all inspections and servicing should be kept in accordance with health and safety legislation.

Industrial sterilisation

This method of sterilisation destroys all bacteria and fungi, and their spores, and viruses. Because this is an industrial process, requiring skilled operators and expensive equipment, it cannot be carried out in the dental surgery. Items such as scalpel blades, sutures, needles, intravenous injection kits and dressings are supplied to be used only once and then disposed off. Manufacturers of such items sterilise these items by exposing them to radiation. Gamma rays obtained from a radioactive source, similar to X-rays, are used.

What is disinfection?

Disinfection can kill or prevent the growth of a variety of microbes; it does not kill spores and is not successful or is unreliable for killing viruses. Because of this disinfection is done only if an item of equipment cannot be sterilised by autoclaving.

A large number of disinfectants that are suitable for use in the dental surgery are available. Disinfectants such as sodium hypochlorite can be used to disinfect work surfaces, impressions and denture work. It is effective against hepatitis B and HIV. Disadvantages of disinfection include:

- Disinfectants may have a limited shelf-life.
- They are often poisonous and need to be handled safely, always following the manufacturer's instructions for dilution and accidental spills or ingestion.

Universal precautions

In order to protect all dental staff from cross-infection and the risks of contamination, and to ensure that patients are protected from cross-infection, the following universal precautions should be adhered to in the dental surgery:

- All members of the dental team should maintain good personal hygiene.
- Handwashing should be carried out at appropriate intervals during the working day.
- Appropriate personal protective equipment (PPE) should be worn.
- Follow approved procedures when dealing with body fluids.
- Follow approved procedures for the de-contamination of all equipment and instruments.
- Follow approved procedures when disposing of contaminated waste products and sharps.
- Ensure that **all** staff are fully vaccinated against hepatitis B and are up to date with all childhood immunisations.
- Make sure that **all** of the dental team members are aware of and understand infection control procedures.

Maintaining cross-infection control in the surgery

The surgery design should ensure maximum cross-infection control, with appropriate ventilation in place (Fig. 4.4). The units should allow ample room for storage of materials, instruments and equipment so that the work surfaces do not become cluttered and untidy. The surgery walls should be easy to clean and without cracks. Floors should not be covered with carpet. A material that can be easily cleaned and is sealed to the floor and walls ensures that debris cannot collect underneath the floor covering or around the edges of the surgery. Any switches, where possible, should be operated by the foot and all cupboard handles, door handles, and light switches should be of a simple design that allows for easy cleaning. Electric wires and tubing should be kept to a minimum, and positioned in such a way as to avoid injury to staff or patients.

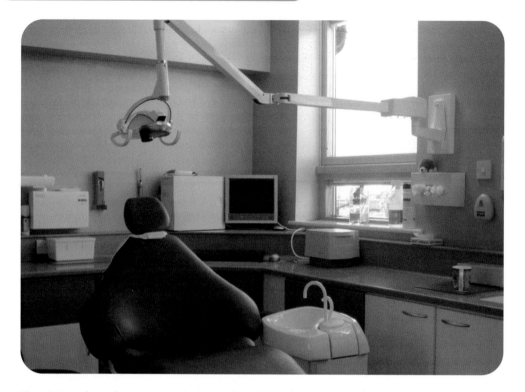

Fig. 4.4 A dental surgery – how it should look.

Personal protection

Dental nurses always need to maintain high levels of personal hygiene, ensuring that their uniform is clean, long hair is tied back off the face and jewellery is kept to the absolute minimum. Shoes should be flat and covered to protect the feet. Protective glasses or visors should be worn to prevent infection from debris entering the eyes. A new pair of disposable gloves should be worn for each patient and disposed of in the clinical waste bin after use. Disposable masks should always be worn when treating a patient and should be changed after each patient.

Protection of dental nurses by immunisation

While working as a dental nurse it is likely that you will come into contact with several diseases. It is therefore essential that you take responsibility to ensure that you have been vaccinated against all such diseases. You need to be aware of when you were vaccinated against each disease and if vaccinations need to be updated through life (Table 4.1). Dental nurses who have not been vaccinated or maintained vaccinations should not be working in the dental surgery.

Table 4.1 Some vaccination schedules

Measles, mumps, rubella (MMR)	Usually received during childhood
Tuberculosis (TB)	Received at approximately 14–15 years of age, after a negative result of Heaf's test
Tetanus	Received during childhood. Booster doses required throughout life to maintain immunity
Poliomyelitis (polio)	Received during childhood
Pertussis (whooping cough)	Received during childhood
Diphtheria	Received during childhood
Hepatitis B	All dental nurses need to receive this vaccination. After a course of three separate injections a blood test needs to be done to ensure that antibodies are present. A booster every 5 years is required to maintain immunity

Handwashing

The dental nurse, as well as all other members of the dental team, must always carry out handwashing following the guidelines set by the General Dental Council and Health and Safety regulators. All dental practices should make available the recommended equipment and materials for correct handwashing procedures to be carried out. This equipment should include a suitable skin cleanser, disposable paper towels, handles on taps that can be operated by the elbows, emollient cream to be used to prevent dry or cracked skin, and suitable waterproof dressings to cover any skin wounds or cuts. The dental nurse must always ensure the following:

- Before washing hands all jewellery (rings, watches, bracelets) must have been removed.
- Fingernails have been kept short and clean.

- Nail varnish should not be worn.

- Handwashing should be performed for at least 30 seconds, in a careful and methodical manner, washing all fingers, hands, wrists and the lower arm.

- When rinsing the hands, water should be allowed to run from hand to elbow, so re-contamination does not take place.

- Hands and arms should be fully dried using disposable paper towels.

- A fresh pair of disposable gloves should be worn, as protection after each handwash has been completed.

- Hand creams or emollients should be used to care for the skin, thus protecting the skin from becoming dry or cracked.

- Any cuts or skin wounds should be covered with dressings.

- Soap dispensers, taps and towel dispensers should be kept clean at all times.

THE DENTAL NURSE'S ROLE

Remember that it is every dental nurse's responsibility to ensure that handwashing is always carried out at the correct frequency, following the correct procedure to maintain cross-infection control.

Preparation of the workplace

At the beginning of the day

At the beginning of each day the dental nurse needs to adopt a regimen to ensure that the surgery and equipment are thoroughly clean and prepared at the start of each session. All work surfaces should be washed with a suitable enzyme-based detergent and a disposable cloth or napkin. Beginning with the highest surfaces, the dental nurse should clean:

- the light, cupboard tops and shelving
- worktops and cupboard surfaces

- chair and bracket table
- aspirator unit and connections
- handpiece cart, connector leads and counters
- spittoon.

Disposable cloths or napkins should be disposed of in the clinical waste bin after use. Air and water lines should be flushed through for three minutes. The dental nurse should also check that clinical waste bags are placed ready in foot-controlled bins, and that the sharps container is not over-full and has not become damaged. If it has it should be replaced.

Plastic disposable covers should be placed on the light handles, 3-in-1 syringe body and bracket table. Disposable covers should also be placed on the headrest of the dental chair. All covers should be changed after each patient.

It is also vitally important for the dental nurse to ensure that each piece of equipment is fully working, and that the autoclave reservoir is filled and a test cycle completed and recorded, complying with the manufacturer's instructions. The surgery should be fully stocked in readiness for the day's procedures, and patients' notes, X-rays and lab work should be ready and checked before the session begins.

During a patient's treatment

The dental nurse should always wear a disposable mask, gloves and glasses while patients are being treated and ensure that the patient is supplied with and wearing protective glasses and a bib. The surgery should be well ventilated when patients are being treated. A safety device should be used to re-sheath syringe needles, and all dental instruments and equipment should be handled carefully and correctly to avoid needle-stick injury.

Disposable gloves that get punctured should be replaced straight away. All work surfaces should be tidied and remain clutter free during a patient's treatment. Any spillages should be dealt with straight away, following the correct procedures.

Following a patient's treatment

Once the patient has left the surgery, the dental nurse needs to prepare the surgery for the next patient. Before doing so the dental nurse needs to ensure that all instruments and the handpieces, scaler tips, etc, are thoroughly cleaned by scrubbing with a detergent to remove all visible debris. Instruments are then placed in an ultrasonic bath to remove any remaining smaller particles. Handpieces should not be put into an ultrasonic bath, but rinsed following the manufacturer's instructions.

ALL WASTE ITEMS SHOULD BE DISPOSED OF CORRECTLY

- Needles, cartridges, sharps – in the sharps bin.
- Cotton-wool balls, tissues, rubber dam, disposable 3-in-1 tips, aspirator tips, saliva injectors – in the clinical waste bin.
- Body fluids, swabs – in the clinical waste bin.
- Waste amalgam – in the amalgam safe or sealed container under water.

All work surfaces, the handpiece couplings, aspirator attachments, bracket table and chair should be cleaned and disinfected. Any impressions taken should be rinsed and disinfected before sending to the dental laboratory. The spittoon should be rinsed and then cleaned. Any materials, cements and specialised equipment should be put back into a drawer or cupboard.

Sterilisation and storage

Once all the debris has been removed from dental instruments and handpieces they can be placed on autoclave trays. Extraction forceps, handpieces and ultrasonic scaler tips are placed in open sterilisation pouches on the autoclave tray. All instruments and equipment should be evenly spaced on the trays to allow sterilisation.

When using an autoclave the manufacturer's instructions should always be followed fully. As previously discussed, there are two types of autoclave in regular use, both of which ensure that all pathogenic organisms and spores are killed once the sterilisation cycle has been completed. Both autoclaves heat to 134°C, holding the temperature for 3 minutes under 2.25 bar pressure. The cycle, from the time the autoclave is switched on until it switches off, is about 20 minutes depending on the model of autoclave. Non-vacuum autoclaves can hold several trays of laid-out instruments for each autoclave cycle. Vacuum autoclaves, which work under vacuum, are suitable for wrapped instruments.

At the end of the day

Again it is essential that the dental nurse adopt a regimen or procedure for maintaining cross-infection control at the end of the day after all planned treatments have taken place. The regimen should include:

- The correct disposal of waste.

- Cleaning and disinfection of all work surfaces, cupboards, unit, dental chair and light.

- Draining the autoclave chamber and water reservoir.

- Rinsing the spittoon for at least two minutes and running water through the handpiece couplings and 3-in-1 syringes.

- Using a recommended disinfectant, flushing through the spittoon, aspirator system, water lines and drainage following the equipment manufacturer's instructions.

- Ensuring that all equipment is switched off, unplugged and stored away.

- Ensuring that all clinical waste bags are secured and ready for collection by a waste company for incineration.

- Checking that the sharps container if three-quarters full is closed and ready for collection, and a new sharps container is ready for use.

Any special waste such as X-ray processing solutions and any irritant, toxic, or corrosive substances should be collected by authorised contractors. Before being taken away they should be placed in rigid puncture-proof containers.

Preparing the surgery for known carriers of the hepatitis B virus

The dental team should adopt the principle of avoiding contact with the patient's blood to avoid infection with the hepatitis B virus. In this instance, the following additional precautions should be adopted:

- Always try to book in the patient who is a hepatitis B carrier to be treated at the end of the day. This will allow the dental nurse additional time to carry out cross-infection control procedures.

- When preparing the surgery remove all unnecessary equipment and materials, storing them away in cupboards, so that they do not come into contact with any instruments, equipment and materials necessary for the procedure.

- Ensure that light switches, handpiece couplings, aspirator 3-in-1 tubing and the handles on the operating light are covered by plastic sheets or Clingfilm.

- Try wherever possible to use disposable items, bibs, aspirator tips, and 3-in-1 tips. Matrix bands and burs should be disposed of after use.

- Ensure that staff who are involved with the patient's treatment are fully up to date with hepatitis B vaccinations and blood tests, and pregnant staff are replaced by another member of staff.

- The dental nurse must always take great care to avoid needle-stick injuries, taking extra time when handling instruments, equipment and sharp objects – always handling them with care.

- A carrier patient who requires surgical procedures, extractions or deep scaling, or a patient in whom the hepatitis B virus is active, should be referred to hospital and not treated at the surgery.

Sharps injuries

Every dental nurse will come into contact with, and be expected to handle, a range of sharp items required for each dental procedure. These items include:

- needles
- cartridges

- scalpel blades
- sutures
- scaler tips
- burs
- dental hand instruments.

To ensure that injuries do not occur, it is essential that each item is handled correctly. Each dental practice should ensure that all staff follow a safety protocol. All new members of staff should be adequately trained in the safe handling of all types of equipment and instruments where sharps injuries could occur.

Occasionally sharps injuries do occur. A sharps injury is often called a 'needle-stick injury' and it refers to all instances when the surface of the skin has been cut or punctured by a sharp item of equipment or dental instrument. It is essential that if such injuries occur the correct procedure is followed by the person who has suffered the injury:

1 Stop work immediately and attend to the wound straight away. Inform the dentist straight away.

2 Do not suck the wound. Encourage bleeding by squeezing the wound (milking the wound).

3 Rinse the area under running water.

4 Dry the injured area with a paper towel and cover the area with a waterproof dressing.

5 Enter the injury in the accident book giving a full account of what happened.

6 If the injury has been the result of handling a contaminated item (used on a patient), then a note should be made of the patient's details and the patient's medical history should be checked.

7 If the patient is a known or suspected HIV carrier, a blood test and emergency treatment will be needed straight away. Contact the consultant microbiologist at your local hospital immediately.

KEY TERMS

Cross-infection	Transfer of infection from one person to another; in the dental surgery it can be transferred as shown in Fig. 4.3 (see p. 73)
Infection	Transmission of a disease into a body by micro-organisms (bacteria, viruses and fungi spores)
Sterilisation	Recommended process to destroy bacteria, viruses, fungi, spores, etc. Carried out by autoclaving or gamma irradiation
Pathogenic	Capable of producing disease
Non-pathogenic	Incapable of producing disease
Asepsis	The absence of living pathogenic organisms

5 Oral Health

5: Oral Health

The four important messages of oral health

1 Effective tooth brushing

Brush your teeth properly with a small multi-tufted nylon toothbrush and interdental toothbrushes. Change your toothbrush every few months or as soon as the bristle start to splay. This is also a form of primary prevention that enables the individual to keep their teeth clean and maintain the periodontal health of their mouth.

The correct tooth brushing technique is when all the plaque is removed. The most effective method is to begin at one corner of the mouth and work your way towards the other side. This should be done on the outer and inner surfaces as well as the biting surfaces for the upper and lower jaws. The toothbrush should be held at a 45 degrees so the bristles are then sweeping the plaque away from the sulcul within the gingival margin. This is called the Bass technique. There are several other techniques but this is the most effective. Care must be taken not to scrub horizontally as this can cause abrasion and gum recession.

Disclosing tablets can be used to check on the thoroughness of cleaning. Interdental brushes are small filaments which clean the spaces between the teeth. These are manufactured in different sizes and shapes to suit a variety of interproximal spaces.

2 A healthy diet that is low in extrinsic sugar

Reduce the amount of sugar in your diet and restrict any sugary snacks and drinks to meal times. This is an important form of primary prevention for everyone. By reducing the amount of sugar in your diet you will reduce the incidence of caries.

3 Regular visits to the dentist.

Visit your dentist every 6 – 12 months. By doing this the above issues will be kept in check and early cavities and signs of periodontal problems can be discovered before any severe problems arise.

4 Fluoride supplements

Check with your local water supplier to check whether or not fluoride is added to your drinking water then consult your dentist or hygienist for advice on supplements. Fluoride is beneficial as it will strengthen the enamel. Systemic fluoride is beneficial when the tooth is in its formative stage so the age of the patient is an important factor when recommending this. Topical fluoride is beneficial when the teeth have formed and erupted. It is not advised that children under 9 years of age use topical fluoride as they will likely swallow the solution.

Oral health education aids

There are several oral health education aids that can be used to help promote your oral health messages. The visual aids will enhance the interest of the person you are talking to. Some examples of teaching aids include:

- Orthodontic appliances on models - useful when discussing the periodontal care of patients wearing such appliances

- Models of teeth and toothbrushes - to shoe your patient how to brush effectively

- Disclosing tablets - to identify missing areas of plaque on the teeth

- Models of crowns, bridges and dentures - to enable you to explain treatment that is involved when discussing specific treatment plans.

Periodontal disease and its control

Plaque and prevention

Plaque is a soft and sticky white deposit that is composed mainly of *Streptococcus mutans* bacteria. It is found in all mouths, and poses a problem only if not cleaned away correctly. Areas of the mouth that are difficult to clean are areas of overcrowded teeth, overhanging restorations and areas of calculus ledges that can trap more plaque deposits. If build-up of plaque is prevented and plaque brushed away regularly, calculous can be avoided.

Chemical removal of plaque involves use of a chlorhexidine mouthwash, but this is not as effective on larger plaque deposits. The disadvantages of chlorhexidine mouthwash are that staining of the enamel can occur and the altered taste sensation. The parotid gland may also swell up, but this is reversible.

Identifying and cleaning away plaque is simpler when using disclosing tablets, as this shows up all areas of plaque deposits, making cleaning easier because the patient can see what has to be cleaned.

Gingivitis

Gingivitis occurs when plaque is left on the teeth surfaces. The gums react by becoming inflamed. This is because the bacteria within the plaque irritate the gingiva and cause the gums to become red and swollen and to bleed easily. A common reaction is for the patients to leave well alone, in the hope that they will heal. The opposite is vital to restore the gums back to health, and the patient must be advised to brush thoroughly, ignoring the bleeding, and the gums will quickly become tighter around the tooth margins, become pink and stippled and stop bleeding. However, there may be other underlying factors, which must not be ignored. These can usually be spotted in the patient's medical history. For example:

- Pregnancy – this can exaggerate the gums' response, making them prone to bleeding. Extra care must be taken with tooth brushing.

- Immunocompromise – patients with diseases affecting their immune system can have an increased response to their gingival condition.

- Blood disorders/conditions such as anaemia and those patients on blood-thinning medications. The disorder must be taken into consideration when the affected patient requires deep scaling or extractions, as excessive bleeding can occur with the latter. Anaemia can cause problems with ulceration.

- Heart conditions/heart murmurs – prophylactic antibiotics, such as amoxicillin should be taken 1 hour before having deep scaling or extractions to prevent any infection around the heart valves.

- Poor nutrition – this can cause the health of the tissues of the gingiva to suffer, as well as the patient's general health.

Periodontal disease

Periodontal disease occurs when gingivitis is not treated and becomes advanced, causing the supporting structures of the tooth to be progressively destroyed and resulting in surrounding bone loss.

Scaling of the teeth is done to remove calculous deposits attached to the teeth. This includes both subgingival and supragingival calculus. Subgingival calculus is when the calculous deposits lie beneath the gingival margin. Supragingival deposits occur above the gingival margin. Calculus is actually calcified plaque deposits that have been hardened by calcium salts within the saliva. Plaque and calculus contain the bacterium, *Streptococcus mutans,* and lactobacilli. This alone does not cause decay. It is only when sugar is also present that the mixture of bacteria and sugar produces the acid that will demineralise the enamel and cause decay.

There are two different types of gingival pocketing (when there is a space between the gum margin and the tooth) that can occur:

- False pocketing – when there is shallow gingival pocket depth, and no supporting bone has been destroyed. This is a reversible condition.

- True pocketing – when the supporting bone structure has been destroyed by residual calculus, and this is irreversible.

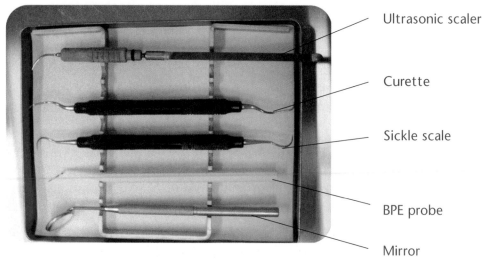

Ultrasonic scaler

Curette

Sickle scale

BPE probe

Mirror

Fig. 5.1 Scaling instruments.

Plaque collects inside the pocket, and if not removed will turn to calculus. The calculus will then gradually destroy the supporting bone.

Regular scaling prevents the build-up of calculous deposits, and also prevents periodontal disease. Several scaling instruments are available for the dentist and/or hygienist to use (Fig. 5.1). The most popular are the sickle scaler and the push scaler. There is also a range of curette scaling instruments, as well as a set of periodontal hoes, which are shaped at varying angles to remove the deposits. An ultrasonic scaler can 'shatter' larger deposits of calculus. This is an electronic instrument that produces ultrasonic vibrations, which loosen the calculus. A water-cooling spray is also part of the apparatus and helps to flush the calculous away.

Prophylactic paste contains more pumice than that of standard toothpaste, and is quite abrasive, so it should not be used too frequently, as the enamel will become scratched. Polishing rubber cups and small brushes can be used in the dental surgery, but must be changed after each polish, and cleaned and sterilised thoroughly, as larger grit particles can remain inside the cups/brushes and over-scratch the next patient's teeth.

Acute necrotising ulcerative gingivitis (ANUG)
ANUG is also known by the following names:

- Vincent's disease
- Acute membranous gingivitis
- Fusospirillosis
- Fusospirochaetal gingivitis
- Necrotising gingivitis
- Phagedenic gingivitis
- Trench mouth.

Causes of ANUG
ANUG is often brought on by stress and/or smoking. It is a progressively painful infection with ulceration, swelling and sloughing off of dead tissue from the mouth and throat due to the spread of infection from the gums. Other causes of this disease include poor oral hygiene, poor nutrition,

and throat, tooth or mouth infections. ANUG is a rare condition which typically affects people between the ages of 15 and 35 years.

In ANUG, there is an abundance of the normal mouth bacteria resulting in infection of the gums. Viruses can also be involved in allowing the bacteria to overgrow. Toxins released by these bacteria irritate the gums causing further infection. If left untreated, the infection leads to ulcer formation which further leads to destruction of the tissues, or trenches (hence the name 'trench mouth'), which affects the support of the teeth. Eventually this can result in the loss of the teeth.

Prevention

Good oral hygiene is important to prevent ANUG, including effective tooth brushing and flossing and regular dental check-ups, and good nutrition and general health. Not smoking is also important, as is taking preventive measures to deal with and alleviate stress.

Symptoms

The symptoms of ANUG are easy to spot and include:

- painful gums
- gums bleeding in response to any pressure or irritation
- reddened gums
- swollen greyish film on the gums
- crater-like ulcers
- foul taste in the mouth
- bad breath.

Treatment

- Antibiotics and sometimes surgery.
- Professional cleaning of the gums is necessary as is irrigation of the mouth with salt water or peroxide solution, which often helps to relieve the symptoms.
- Rest and a balanced diet, and avoiding smoking.
- Eating hot and spicy foods can irritate the mouth, so avoidance of these while undergoing treatment is advised.

Dental caries and its control

Causes of caries

Different types of sugars

There are various types of sugars that come under the heading 'total sugars':

Intrinsic sugars – examples of these are fresh fruit and vegetables. The actual sugar molecules are inside the cells and have naturally formed within the fruit.

Extrinsic sugars – this is where the sugar molecules are outside the cells, and have been added artificially. This group is further divided:

- Milk sugars – lactose is the source of sugar.
- Non-milk sugars, such as table sugar and honey.

Caries

Caries is one of the most common diseases affecting the western world. To be able to control it, you need to understand how it begins.

Bacteria (*Streptococcus mutans*) are normally found in the mouth, and are quite harmless until sugar is introduced and acid is formed. Lactobacilli, which are also found in the mouth, thrive on this acidic environment. It is this acid that causes demineralisation of the enamel surface.

The types of sugar that cause dental caries are extrinsic sugars, such as sucrose and glucose. These are described in further detail below. The acid begins the caries process and, the more often you consume sugars (whether it be in food or liquid form), the more frequently you will create the environment for caries to progress even further. This is commonly referred to as an 'acid attack'. Stephan's curve (Fig 5.2), explains that when sugar is frequently consumed, the normal pH (7) of the mouth will drop, increasing the opportunity for demineralisation to occur (below 5.5). When the pH has an opportunity to rise, more frequently than falling, remineralisation can occur. If decay is already in its early stages, then the tooth may repair. Oral health education is imperative in the prevention further episodes of caries, and the continuing care of the remaining dentition.

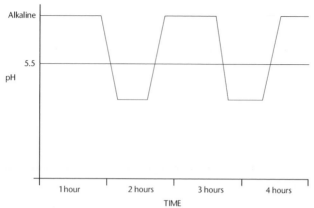

Fig. 5.2 Stephan's curve

The path of caries

Caries will initially break through a point in the enamel surface. It will then 'mushroom' into the dentine below. The caries can then progress fairly rapidly, with only a small mark on the enamel surface visible to the naked eye. As the caries progresses even further, the enamel surface can break through leaving a larger cavity. The patient may be aware of the caries before this stage, as the tooth may be painful or just sensitive to temperature extremes. Caries can attack any tooth surface, but is more prevalent on the occlusal (biting) surface, where the pits and fissures can attract and stagnate sticky sugary foods, and the interproximal surface, which is the space between two adjacent teeth, causing the same problems.

The dentist can spot early carious lesions by radiographs, the naked eye, shadowing of the enamel, pain reporting from the patient and if a sharp dental instrument were to 'stick' on a tooth surface.

Early carious lesions have the appearance of being white chalky marks on the teeth, or as a dark shadow as previously discussed. The chalky appearance is due to the calcium phosphate within the enamel being removed by the acid. More advanced caries will show obvious cavities, with an orange colour if the caries is still active and a much darker appearance if the caries has arrested (no longer active).

Saliva is the body's own natural defence mechanism in helping to prevent caries. Saliva contains mainly water (99%), but the remaining constituents are bicarbonate, calcium and phosphate ions, which, along with the water content help to dilute dietary sugars, assist in neutralising the acids, that help in demineralisation of early carious lesions.

Pulpitis

If the caries is extensive, acute pain may be present and the pulp chamber may be infected, resulting in pulpitis, which can cause an alveolar abscess. The treatment for this is either to progress with antibiotics and a root canal treatment or, if this is not possible, to extract the tooth.

Acute abscess

An abscess is caused by the acute pressure from the infected pulp on the tiny neck of the pulp chamber. This increases the pressure around this area, which constricts the blood vessels and nerve supply, causing death of the pulp. A dental abscess is extremely painful and can cause acute facial swelling. If this is ignored for some time, the swelling can rapidly increase and cause the patient to become pyrexic (raised temperature) and require intravenous antibiotics in hospital.

Chronic abscess

A chronic abscess is self-draining, and there will be a 'sinus' at a point above the infected tooth, which will drain pus on its own, as the pressure increases, and relieve the intense pain. Both types of abscess can go either way, with an acute abscess becoming chronic and a chronic abscess becoming acute. Chronic abscesses are more common in deciduous teeth.

Prevention of caries

Fluoride

Fluoride is a chemical formed by the element fluorine, and is often found naturally in foods such as those containing fish bones and drinks such as beer and tea. Fluoride occurs naturally as **calcium fluoride** in rocks. Fluoride is released when water comes into contact with the rocks. There are some areas of Britain where fluoride occurs naturally, such as Hartlepool, Uttoxeter and areas of Derbyshire. Other areas where it occurs naturally but at lower levels are Essex and Kent. The level of fluoride that provides the most benefit is 1 part per million (ppm). There is no evidence that levels as low as 0.1 ppm or 0.2 ppm provide any benefit to dental health.

When fluoride is artificially added to water, it is in the form of **sodium fluoride** and added at the optimum level of 1 ppm (the level at which decay prevention will be active). The areas of Britain that have artificially added fluoride are south Staffordshire, Warwickshire, Dudley, north Lincolnshire, and more extensively in the West Midlands – Birmingham, Solihull, Sandwell, Walsall, Wolverhampton and Coventry. In the latter regions fluoridation was introduced in the mid-1960s and in the former in the early 1970s.

In a British Association for the Study of Community Dentistry (BASCD) survey, it was found that five-year-old children living in south Staffordshire had the best dental health, with six times less decay than those living in Glasgow, which is a non-fluoridated area. In a further survey of 5–15 year olds, it was shown that 64% of these children had no decay and, on balance, among five-year-olds from social classes IV (small employers and own account workers) and V (lower supervisory and technical occupations) this was reduced to 63%. Adults who have lived in mainly fluoridated areas for most of their lives, had (in the York survey), around 30% fewer decayed, missing or filled (DMF) teeth, while those aged between 45 and 65 in this category had between 40% and 50% more of their own natural teeth.

Other regions of the world that have fluoridated water include several states in the USA (the first fluoridation scheme began in Grand Rapids, Michigan in 1945), Sydney, Melbourne, Auckland, Hong Kong, Dublin, Jerusalem and Tel Aviv.

Dental fluorosis presents in children as pearlescent, small, white flecks within the enamel, but is purely an aesthetic problem. While still a concern, parents can reduce the risk by supervising tooth brushing when their children are still young, making sure that they do not ingest too much toothpaste, particularly if they are also being given fluoride supplements (Table 5.1). The recommended amount of toothpaste is the size of a small pea, and only a small smear is required across the toothbrush for babies. Toothpastes designed specifically for babies and young children contain lower levels of fluoride.

Finally, public support (or not) has been an ongoing issue, and indeed has generated debate, as to whether fluoride should be artificially added to the drinking water supplies in Britain. A poll lead by MORI (Market and Opinion Research International Ltd) in 2000 noted that, in the West Midlands, 71% of people agreed that fluoride should be added, with the highest level of support (78%) being from those aged between the 16 and 24 years.

The cause of decay is, of course, frequent consumption of sugar, so this must be taken into account, particularly with those who disagree with the artificial addition of fluoride to the drinking water supply.

Table 5.1 Recommended fluoride dosages for those not living in an area that has naturally occurring or artificially supplemented fluoride

6 months–3 years	0.25 mg daily
3–6 years	0.5 mg daily
6–12 years	1 mg daily

What is added to water apart from fluoride?

There are several naturally occurring elements and chemicals, that are also added to water, and the list below is for information purposes only. Some are present because they are added at the water treatment stage, but others occur naturally. Up to 4000 trace elements have been found in drinking water throughout the world over the years, but the list below contains some of the most commonly present:

- Chlorine
- Magnesium
- Sodium
- Iron
- Manganese
- Copper
- Aluminium
- Nitrates
- Calcium.

Sulphates, bicarbonates, insecticides and herbicides may also be present.

It should be mentioned that the entire cost of setting up and running water fluoridation met by the National Health Service (NHS), and comparing the cost of around 15 pence per person in the Birmingham area of the UK with the cost of filling or indeed extracting a grossly decayed tooth, fluoride is indeed the cheaper option.

Topical and systemic fluorides

Topical fluoride is a fluoride supplement that goes over the teeth without being ingested (swallowed). An advantage of topical fluoride is that it desensitises the enamel, and can assist in remineralisation of any early carious lesions. Examples of topical fluorides are:

- Fluoride mouthwash
- Fluoride toothpaste
- Fluoride varnishes (Duraphat)
- Fluoride gels (applied by the dentist or hygienist).

After topical fluoride treatments, no food or drink should be consumed for about 1 hour, or the patient should follow the manufacturer's instructions or those given by the dentist or hygienist.

Systemic fluoride is taken on a daily basis from the age of 6 months to 12 years. This is designed to prevent decay by incorporation of fluoride within the developing tooth.

Examples of systemic fluorides are:

- Fluoride tablets
- Fluoride drops.

Medications and sugar

Several medications still contain sugar. The advice is either to read the labels or to ask the pharmacist to check for you. Medications that have to be taken frequently, particularly in children, require checking, as it is the frequency rather than the amount that causes tooth decay.

The COMA Report

The COMA Report (Committee On Medical Aspects of Food Policy) was set up to look at dietary reference values. Terms to know are:

- RDI (recommended daily intake)
- RDA (recommended daily amount)

- EAR (estimated average requirement (mean) of a group from a particular nutrient or for energy)
- RNI (amount of a nutrient that is sufficient for almost all individuals)
- LRNI (amount of a nutrient that is sufficient for only a few individuals. Habitual intakes below the LRNI by an individual will almost certainly be inadequate)
- DRV (dietary reference value – a general term that covers all: EAR, RNI and LRNI).

There have been three COMA reports in 1969, 1979 and 1991. The reports set out in 1969 and 1979 based their recommendations on single figures – RDIs and RDAs. They were set deliberately high, which predisposed to the risk of misuse. The guidelines were set high because they wanted to increase levels of nutrition by recommending that the public consumed more than they needed, trying effectively to avoid malnutrition. To avoid this in the 1991 COMA report, a new set of values, with the DRV based on the requirements and distribution for each nutrient, were used and were set as guidelines rather than recommendations. This also covered both the RDI and the RDA groups. These estimated requirements are taken from a cross-section, whereby the following were assessed:

- Energy
- Fats, sugars, starches, non-polysaccharides, 13 vitamins and 15 types of minerals
- Total sugar and non-milk sugars
- Sodium and salt
- Total fat and saturated fats
- Fibre.

The COMA panel decided that non-milk extrinsic sugars should be limited because of their role in dental caries. It was noted that the frequency of intake of these sugars was a vital point to consider, so the panel agreed that total sugar consumption should be taken into account, and the average consumption of non-milk extrinsic sugars should not exceed 10% of total dietary energy.

Several updates have been made to the COMA report, eg the importance of folic acid in the diet, and the latest addition by the Healthy Eating Policy from McDonald's, which have agreed to comply with the COMA report and reduce saturated fat by 35% and total fat by 12% between 1990 and 2005.

SOME FACTS ABOUT SOME SUGAR SUBSTITUTES

- Sorbitol, mannitol, xylitol and maltitol are sugar alcohols. They occur naturally in fruits and are produced from such sources as dextrose. Xylitol is a sugar alcohol made from a part of birch trees. Sorbitol, mannitol and maltitol are about half as sweet as sucrose. Xylitol has a sweetness equal to sucrose.

- Sucralose is the newest approved sugar substitute and is about 600 times sweeter than sugar. It is extremely stable and does not break down during cooking.

- Acesulfame-K is 200 times sweeter than sugar, is stable during normal temperatures and does not break down in cooking.

- Aspartame is 200 times sweeter than sugar and contains two amino acids (phenylalanine and aspartic acid). It has no after-taste, but cannot be used in baking as it breaks down. Brand names are NutraSweet and Equal.

- Saccharine has been around the longest and is 200 times sweeter than sugar. It is very stable in foods but does impart a bitter after-taste.

Fissure sealants

Fissure sealants have been commercially available for dentists since the early 1970s, although they were actually designed as far back as the 1950s and 1960s. Fissure sealants are plastic resins designed to seal the natural pits and fissures of the teeth (Fig. 5.3), where food can collect and stagnate. The resin flows over the occlusal surface of the molar teeth and helps to prevent decay on that particular surface.

Fissure sealants are normally used when there is a greater change of decay, and should be used in conjunction with a more enhanced plan of decay prevention.

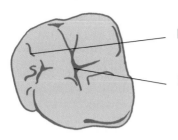

Fissures

Pit

Fig. 5.3 Occlusal view of a molar showing pits and fissures.

Preparing the tooth/teeth for a fissure sealant

A totally dry mouth is essential. Dry guards can be used against the salivary glands next to the cheeks, to help absorb the flow of saliva. Aspiration is also important to keep the area free from moisture, otherwise the fissure sealant will not be retained.

There are two different types of fissure sealant: chemically cured or cured by an ultraviolet (UV) light. Care must be taken with a UV shield to protect your eyes when using the light.

Plasma light can be artificially produced from a xenon short arc lamp powered at high voltage and a specific frequency. The Apollo 95 is tuned to produce energy of the wavelength required to activate the camphoro-quinone nitiator that is used in many dental products. The difference between the Apollo 95 and a conventional light is that ten times the amount of light is produced in this wave length, but less produced at other wavelengths. The effect is to produce a high energy light source which is capable of curing light-cured dental materials in a matter of seconds.

THE DENTAL NURSE'S ROLE – ORAL HEALTH

- Retrieve the patient notes and identify the procedure.

- Prepare the surgery with all the required instruments, materials and medicaments.

- Check patients' medical history in accordance with the procedure they are having.

- Be aware of health and safety at all times, and of personal protective equipment (PPE) for all staff and patients, to help minimise cross-infection, and aspirate when required.

- Be able to anticipate the next stage of any given treatment, so that you can prepare and provide adequate and professional continuity in the treatment plan.

- Thoroughly clean and clear away instruments, medicaments and materials. Wipe surfaces with isopropyl alcohol or similar.

- Sterilise when required in a regularly serviced autoclave – keeping clean and dirty instruments away from each other, as well as dirty gloves from the previous procedure that can contaminate 'clean' gloves.

KEY TERMS

Fluoride

Fluoride	Both a naturally occurring and an artificially added element in drinking water to enable the enamel to become more resistant to dental caries
Systemic fluoride	Fluoride ingested within the body, eg fluoridated water, fluoride tablets/drops
Topical fluoride	Fluoride used on the surfaces of the teeth, eg fluoride varnish/mouthwash and toothpaste

Fissure sealants

Stagnating area	Area where plaque and food are more likely to accumulate in the mouth, such as overhanging amalgam ledges and/or overcrowded teeth
Interproximal area	Area between two teeth
Pits and fissures of teeth	Naturally occurring grooves on the occlusal surface of the molar and premolar teeth

Other terms

Stephan's curve	Diagram used to demonstrate the effect that sugar has in causing caries
Demineralisation	When the calcium and phosphates are drawn out of the enamel prisms within the teeth (which can be caused by both frequent sugar intake and problems with enamel erosion, frequent acidic food and drink consumption, and frequent vomiting)
Remineralisation	When the calcium and phosphates within the enamel recover sufficiently, following demineralisation

6 Clinical Assessment of Oral Health

6: Clinical Assessment of Oral Health

What is a clinical assessment?

Clinical assessment of a patient's oral health is an examination of the condition of the extraoral and intraoral soft tissues, dentition and periodontal tissues. It is an opportunity for any medical problems – past, present or ongoing – to be recorded in a patient's notes and to be considered when planning treatments. The assessment also creates the opportunity for the dentist to assess the position and function of teeth.

Clinical assessments are carried out for all new patients who attend a practice and at all recall appointments, although it can also be said that each time a patient attends the practice for treatment the dentist will observe and examine the oral cavity and investigate further any means of concern. The main purpose of a clinical assessment is to:

- identify any problems
- carry out further investigations
- make a diagnosis
- formulate an agreed treatment plan
- promote the prevention of cavities and periodontal disease to the patient.

Early detection of any problems with the hard or soft tissues of the mouth can prevent the condition from becoming more serious.

Dental records

Under the NHS regulations a dental practitioner is required to keep adequate patient records. These records are regarded as legally valid documents. Patient records hold a large amount of information about each patient, including personal details, medical history and past dental history.

Personal details

Patient records should be written correctly to avoid errors or insufficient information relating to the patient, the treatment or a medical history.

A PATIENT'S RECORD BUILDS UP A CLEAR PICTURE OF THE PERSON IN QUESTION

- Any problems with a patient's general health.

- Medication taken, including dosage and frequency.

- Detailed past dental history of past assessments, treatment required and treatment completed.

- Personal information, if the patient is in receipt of any benefits, if they are a nervous patient, failed appointments, if they have refused treatment in the past, any special preferences for times or days when they prefer to attend the practice.

- A full dental history.

- Details of dental fees paid or any unpaid accounts.

It may be part of your duties when assisting the dentist actually to record information in a patient's dental record. It is therefore essential that the patient gives you all the information, and you record it accurately and completely.

Medical history

A medical history needs to be taken at every oral assessment appointment and should be updated frequently to allow for any changes in the patient's condition or medication to be entered in the patient notes. Many dental practices now give all patients a printed medical questionnaire to complete. They also remind patients of the importance of informing the dentist if there are any changes to their medical history or present condition by printing a statement on the practice appointment cards, or by displaying notices in the waiting rooms and reception areas.

Medical questionnaires

Medical questionnaires can take many forms and ask the patient a range of questions:

- Are you attending or receiving any medical treatment?
- Are you taking any medication – what is it and how often do you take it?
- Do you smoke?
- Do you drink alcohol; if yes how much do you drink?
- Do you have any allergies?
- Are you pregnant?
- Have you had any operations, for what and when?
- Is there any history of heart problems/rheumatic fever/liver problems/high blood pressure/kidney disease/epilepsy/ diabetes/asthma/hay fever/respiratory problems/fainting/bleeding excessively/bad reactions to local or general anaesthetic/arthritis?
- Have you taken steroids in the past two years?
- Are you HIV positive?
- Do you or have you recently taken antidepressants?
- Do you carry a medical warning card?

Patients are asked to complete the medical questionnaire, and then sign and date it. For children, a parent is asked to complete and sign the medical questionnaire on their behalf. It is also important to identify those patients who may not be able to complete a medical questionnaire by themselves. Patients who do not speak or read English, patients who have problems with their sight or patients who may have dyslexia will need assistance to enable a full and accurate medical history to be taken. Details from the medical questionnaire are passed to the dentist, who updates the patient notes. Completed medical questionnaires are usually kept with the patient notes, so that they can be referred to.

Past dental history

This includes all past dental problems and past dental treatment, together with a full charting history, radiographs taken, or study models. Other information may include previous difficulties with extractions, excessive bleeding, allergy to dental materials and poor response to local anaesthetics.

All patient records should be stored securely at all times. The Data Protection Act obliges all dentists to register under the Act if they hold patient records in the practice computer system and if manual records are kept. The Act protects the patient's right to privacy, thereby ensuring that a patient's records are not disclosed to unauthorised people or sources.

At any time the patient has the right to see their own records and to amend any inaccuracies on them. Patient records should be kept for at least 11 years and afterwards they should be destroyed by incineration, so that all important information is irretrievable.

ROLE OF THE DENTAL NURSE IN PREPARING THE SURGERY, EQUIPMENT, INSTRUMENTS AND MATERIALS FOR CLINICAL ASSESSMENT

- Ensure that the surgery is fully cleaned and operational before preparing for the clinical assessment.

- The patient records, together with and including past medical and dental history, charting history, radiographs, photographs, and study models, should be available.

- A range of instruments, materials and equipment is required for a thorough examination of the hard and soft tissues of the oral cavity and includes mouth mirror, probe and periodontal probe.

- Alginate impression material, together with a suitable selection of upper and lower impression trays, fixer, mixing bowl, spatula, powder and water measures, laboratory bag and laboratory instruction form.

- Mouthwash bib and protective glasses for the patient.

- Additional materials to be made available include pulp tester, ethyl chloride, gutta percha to test tooth vitality, camera.

Radiographs (intraoral or extraoral) aid in detecting dental cavities, bone loss and periodontal disease, diagnosing hard tissue lesions (bone cysts, tumours), position of erupted and unerupted teeth, and detecting supernumerary teeth. The camera is used by the dentist to take photographs to record various aspects of the patient's dentition, bite, views of soft tissues, and before and after views of dental treatment. Study models may be necessary for occlusal analysis where full mouth treatment may be necessary for orthodontic assessment, to assess the position and function of the teeth.

The electric pulp tester is used to determine the degree of vitality of a tooth. The electric pulp tester works by sending an increasing current into the tooth, or teeth, being tested until a patient indicates a sensation, which is then recorded in the patient notes. Usually several healthy teeth are tested as well as the suspect tooth, which enables the operator to establish the normal response of a healthy tooth before acknowledging the response of the suspect tooth (Table 6.1). Other methods of testing teeth vitality are with ethyl chloride (cold stimulus) and heated gutta percha (hot stimulus).

Table 6.1 Meaning of responses to a pulp tester

Normal response	Indicates a healthy pulp
Increased response	Indicates early pulpitis
Reduced response	Indicates that the pulp is dying
No response	Indicates that the pulp is dead

THE DENTAL NURSE'S ROLE IN PROVIDING SUPPORT FOR THE DENTIST AND ASSISTING THE DENTIST DURING THE ORAL HEALTH ASSESSMENT

Dental nurses should be fully aware of their duties throughout the clinical assessment to maintain patient care and comfort throughout the procedure, and to complement the actions of the dentist by anticipating their needs and acting accordingly. With these duties in mind they should be able:

- To monitor, support and reassure the patient throughout the appointment.

- To be able to prepare and supply the dentist with instruments, equipment and materials as required throughout the procedures.

- To be able to identify and understand the surfaces of teeth, and classification of cavities to record successfully the charting of teeth.

- To be familiar with and understand how to record periodontal conditions and charting.

- To be able to make accurate clinical records as required throughout the procedure; such notes need to be full and concise.

- To explain to the patient when other appointments need to be arranged to carry out further treatment, and what the treatments are.

Methods of recording information from the assessment of the patient's oral health

The first assessment that the dentist will carry out is a general assessment of the patient. This may include:

- How responsive the patient is to any questions that may be asked.
- If the patient has problems communicating with the dentist and dental nurse.
- Does the patient have any mobility problems?
- The patient's level of fear and anxiety.

The findings of this assessment are recorded in the patient notes. Identifying and recorded details of this assessment will assist members of the dental team to treat the patient suitably at future dental appointments.

The dentist will then carry out an assessment of the extraoral soft tissues. This assessment is carried out to detect and record any abnormalities.

Extraoral assessment

This assessment involves the examination of the external facial appearance, concentrating on skin colour, shape of the face, skin blemishes, condition of the lips and examination of the lymph nodes.

Skin colour – Skin colour, texture and tone vary from one person to another, but if patients suddenly become pale or look paler than they usually do this may indicate illness, fear or anxiety. Patients who have an unnatural ruddy skin colour may be suffering from hypertension.

Skin blemishes – Any blemishes of the skin will be examined, especially moles. Any mole with ragged edges that are raised or bleed should be further investigated, as this could prove to be a melanoma, which would need urgent further treatment.

Lymph nodes – On examination any enlargement of the lymph nodes indicates that the body is fighting infection, or may indicate other disease processes.

Lips – The presence of cold sores would be recorded in the patient notes. Bluish-tinged lips could be a result of chronic heart failure.

Intraoral assessment

All soft tissues inside the mouth are examined. These include the tongue, floor of the mouth, hard and soft palate, throat, tonsils, and labial, buccal and sulcus mucosae. The colour, texture and moisture levels of each surface are examined. Any swellings or abnormalities will be further examined as these can indicate problems that may require urgent or further treatment.

An important role performed by the dental nurse is accurately to record the findings of the oral assessment, in such a manner as is universally recognised by all members of the dental profession.

Dental charting

During the assessment of the patient's oral health, each surface of each tooth is examined and the findings are recorded in a chart, which forms part of the patient notes. The chart shows a simplified version of the surfaces of each tooth in a full dentition and its number (Fig. 6.1).

UR8 UR7 UR6 UR5 UR4 UR3 UR2 UR1 UL1 UL2 UL3 UL4 UL5 UL6 UL7 UL8

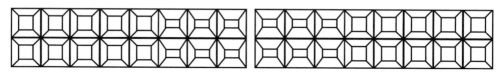

LR8 LR7 LR6 LR5 LR4 LR3 LR2 LR1 LL1 LL2 LL3 LL4 LL5 LL6 LL7 LL8

Fig. 6.1 A dental chart.

The centre-line of the teeth corresponds with the centre-line on the dental chart. Each quadrant of the chart corresponds with the quadrant of the patient's oral cavity as you look at them (Table 6.2). From the centre-line, each tooth is recorded by number: 1 in each quadrant is the tooth next to the centre-line and thereafter the teeth numbers are 2, 3, 4, 5, 6, 7, 8 from the front to the back of the mouth (Table 6.3). In the deciduous dentition, each tooth is identified and referred to by a letter. Again each tooth is identified from the centre-line (Table 6.4).

Table 6.2 The quadrants in the oral cavity

Upper right	Upper left
Lower right	Lower left

Table 6.3 Tooth numbers from the centre-line in each quadrant

8 7 6 5 4 3 2 1	1 2 3 4 5 6 7 8
8 7 6 5 4 3 2 1	1 2 3 4 5 6 7 8

Table 6.4 Deciduous teeth notation

E D C B A	A B C D E
E D C B A	A B C D E

On a dental chart the shape of each tooth is simplified and designed to show each surface of the tooth. In both the deciduous and permanent dentition the incisors and canines in the upper and lower quadrants appear as shown in Fig. 6.2. Molars and premolars in both arches appear as shown in Fig. 6.3.

Fig. 6.2 Upper anterior teeth (centrals, incisors and canines)

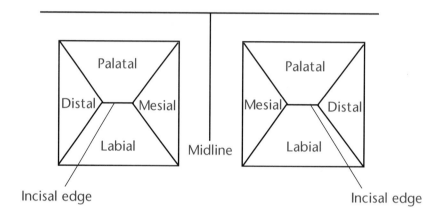

Upper posterior teeth (pre-molars, molars)

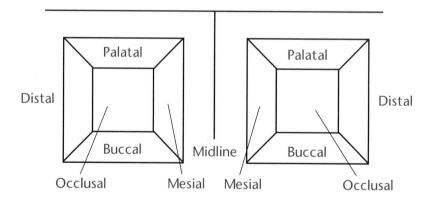

Fig. 6.3 Lower anterior teeth (centrals, incisors, lateral incisors, canines)

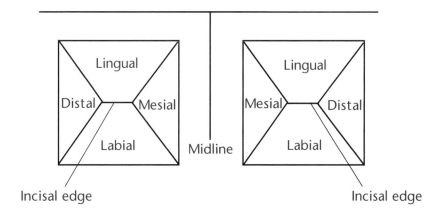

Lower anterior teeth (pre-molars, molars)

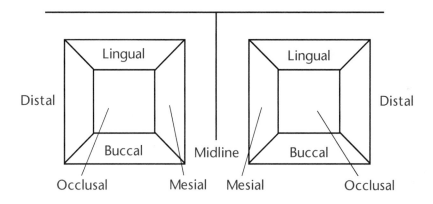

To enable each member of the dental team to read and understand a patient's dental chart it is very important that the dental nurse is able to chart all past dental treatment and treatment required, using the recognised notation. Table 6.5 shows recognised notation used universally to allow all members of the dental team to understand a patient's dental chart.

Table 6.5 Standard notations for dental charting

x	Recently extracted tooth
≠	Tooth to be extracted
Ⓜ	Tooth missing
→	Space closed
#	Fracture
UE	Unerupted tooth
PE	Partially erupted tooth
I	Implant
PJC	Porcelain jacket crown
FGC	Full-gold crown
RF	Root-filled tooth
FS	Fissure sealed
FBC	Full-bonded crown
GI	Gold inlay
RCT	Root canal therapy
BA	Bridge abutment
BP	Bridge pontic
PC	Post crown
ꝯ	Rotated tooth
PV	Porcelain veneer
CM	Composite filling
TM	Temporary filling

FDI (International Dental Federation) system of charting

This is a two-digit method of charting (Table 6.6), whereby each quadrant and each tooth are identified by numbers.

Permanent dentition

- Upper right quadrant is known as 1
- Upper left quadrant is known as 2
- Lower left quadrant is known as 3
- Lower right quadrant is known as 4.

Table 6.6 The FDI system for permanent teeth

Quadrant 1	Quadrant 2
Quadrant 4	Quadrant 3

Each tooth is then identified by a number: 1 is the central incisor in each quadrant, 2 is the lateral incisor, 3 is the canine, 4 is the first premolar, 5 is the second premolar, 6 is the first molar, 7 is the second molar and 8 is the third molar (Table 6.7).

Table 6.7 The FDI system of numbering permanent teeth

18 17 16 15 14 13 12 11	21 22 23 24 25 26 27 28
48 47 46 45 44 43 42 41	31 32 33 34 35 36 37 38 39

Deciduous dentition:

- Upper right quadrant is known as 5
- Upper left quadrant is known as 6
- Lower left quadrant is known as 7
- Lower right quadrant is known as 8 (Table 6.8).

Each deciduous tooth is also identified by a number, beginning at the midline: central incisor is 1, lateral incisor is 2, canine is 3, first molar is 4 and second molar is 5 (Table 6.9).

Table 6.8 The FDI system for deciduous teeth

Quadrant 5	**Quadrant 6**
Quadrant 8	**Quadrant 7**

Table 6.9 The FDI system of numbering deciduous teeth

55 45 35 25 15	61 62 63 64 65
85 84 83 82 81	71 72 73 74 75

Assessment of the periodontal tissues

The assessment of the periodontal tissues is carried out as part of the overall oral health assessment. This is because the periodontal ligament and alveolar bone can be affected in periodontal disease, which in severe cases can affect oral health owing to the destruction of these supporting structures.

It is vitally important that the condition of the supporting tissues is examined and recorded. This assessment is known as 'basic periodontal examination' (BPE). A special probe, which has graduated markings on it, is used to probe the periodontal pockets, measuring the depth in millimetres of any pockets present. The findings of the examination are then coded and recorded on a BPE chart (Tables 6.10 and 6.11).

Table 6.10 BPE coding

Code	Description
0	Healthy gingival tissue, no bleeding
1	Coloured area of probe visible, no calculus or defective margins
2	Plaque, supra- and subgingival calculus detected. Pocket less than 3.5 mm deep
3	Coloured area of probe partially visible. Pocket depth less than 5.5 mm deep
4	Coloured area of probe not visible. Pocket depth more than 6.0 mm deep
*	Bone loss and/or recession. Pocket depth 7.0 mm or more

Table 6.11 Charting according to the BPE

Upper right posterior teeth 3	Upper anterior teeth 0	Upper left posterior teeth 3
Lower right posterior teeth 2	Lower anterior teeth 1	Lower left posterior teeth 2

The presence of plaque and its extent may be noted during the periodontal assessment and the standard of the patient's oral hygiene can be graded and recorded. The mobility of teeth due to loss of bone support can be graded as follows:

1 Side-to-side movement of less than 2 mm

2 Side-to-side movement of more than 2 mm

3 Vertical movement also possible.

7 Dental Radiography

7: Dental Radiography

Radiographs are used in dentistry to aid in the diagnosis of dental problems. Radiographs can be taken for the following reasons:

- To detect dental caries
- To detect periapical and periodontal abscesses
- To detect overhanging restorations
- Used as a diagnostic aid in endodontic treatment
- To detect cysts and fractures
- To detect the position of unerupted teeth and supernumeraries (extra teeth)
- To check the roots and positions of teeth before extraction
- To check bone levels
- To check the position of jaws in relation to each other and the skull and temporomandibular jaw (TMJ).

Types of radiograph used in dentistry

Two types of radiographs are used in dentistry.

Intraoral

These radiographs are taken by putting the film inside the mouth. They can be:

Horizontal bitewing – Used to detect interproximal caries and caries underneath existing fillings.

Vertical bitewing – Used to detect the level of bone in posterior teeth.

Periapical (Fig. 7.1) – Used for any tooth to check for periapical or periodontal abscess, for diagnostic use in endodontic treatment, and for root fractures and the position of the roots of individual teeth.

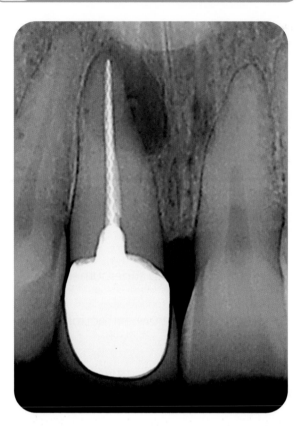

Fig. 7.1 A periapical radiograph.

Occlusal (Fig. 7.2) – Slightly larger than a periapical radiograph, this is used to detect the position of unerupted canine and premolar teeth and the presence of any supernumeraries.

Fig. 7.2 An occlusal radiograph.

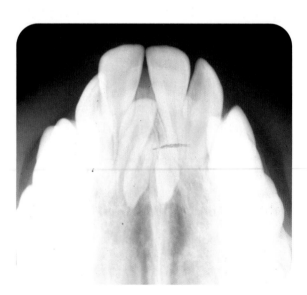

There are two different techniques that can be used to take a periapical radiograph depending on the situation.

Paralleling technique (Fig. 7.3)
This is when the film is placed directly parallel to the tooth, so that the image seen is exactly the same size as the tooth. This is useful for endodontic treatments when the dentist can take an exact measurement of the root canal.

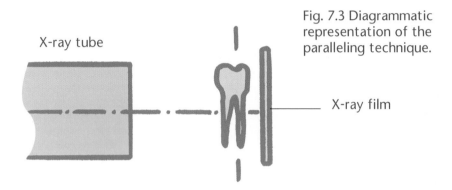

Fig. 7.3 Diagrammatic representation of the paralleling technique.

X-ray tube

X-ray film

Bisecting angle technique (Fig. 7.4)
It is not always possible to get the film exactly parallel to the patient's tooth as the mouth may be too small or the patient may gag easily and not be able to accommodate the film very well. In this case the bisecting angle technique needs to be used. An imaginary line bisects the angle between the film and the long axis of the tooth. The x-ray tube is positioned to take the x-ray at a right angle to this imaginary line.

Fig. 7.4 Diagrammatic representation of the bisecting technique.

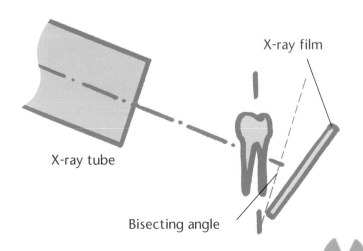

X-ray film

X-ray tube

Bisecting angle

Extra-oral

Orthopantomogram (OPG, or dental panoramic tomograph (DPT)) (Fig. 7.5) – This gives a view of all the teeth and jaws. It is used to assess bone levels in periodontal disease, the position of unerupted teeth and position of the inferior dental nerve, to detect jaw fractures and to assess the position of the TMJs.

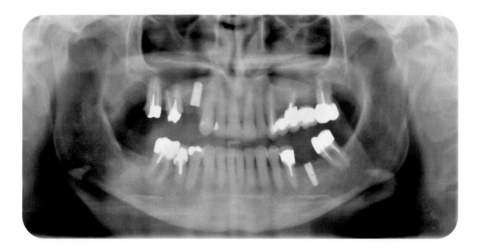

Fig. 7.5 An orthopantomogram.

Lateral cephalogram – This gives a lateral (side view) of the jaws, either the right or the left, depending on which side the radiograph is taken. It is used in orthodontics to see the relationship of the upper and lower jaws in malocclusions.

It is important when patients are having radiographs taken that they remove any dentures or removable orthodontic appliances. If they are having an extraoral radiograph, any ear or nose piercing must be removed as these can distort the image of the radiograph.

Intensifying screens sandwich the film and are used in extraoral radiographs to reduce the amount of radiation exposure needed by increasing the speed of the process to produce the image of the exposed radiograph. If these screens were not used the radiation exposure would be dangerously high.

Ionising radiation

When radiographs are taken it involves the use of ionising radiation, which is a type of electromagnetic radiation. X-rays produce a lot of energy so that they are able to pass through tissue. When a radiograph is taken some X-rays are absorbed by the tissues, ie teeth and bones, and some pass through or bounce off the tissue as scattered radiation. X-rays also release energy which can cause tissue damage. Tissue damage occurs in the chromosomes of cells causing them to die. This is why the dosage of X-rays must be kept to a minimum. There must be a definite need to take a radiograph and the radiograph that will give the best diagnosis with the minimum of exposure must be used.

The X-rays form a latent image on the exposed radiograph. This means that the image cannot be seen until it has been developed. The denser the tissue the less radiation is allowed to pass through so more will be absorbed and appear whiter on the radiograph once developed, compared with something less dense such as pulp.

Processing of dental radiographs

In order to view a radiograph it must be processed using the correct procedure.

Manual processing

This must be done under darkroom conditions, ie where all light has been blocked out except for a red safety light which allows you to see what you are doing. There must also be a warning device outside the room to prevent people coming into the room when you are developing a film:

- Wipe the film packaging to remove any saliva which could contaminate it and remove the film from its packaging (Fig. 7.6).

- Place the film into a developing solution for time specified. The image will develop on the film.

- Rinse the film in water and place into a fixing solution to fix the image to the film. The film is then rinsed in water again to remove any excess fixer.

- Dry the film on a hanger. The film can be viewed at this point.

If the solutions are used frequently they will need changing more regularly as the developer becomes exhausted. When the solutions deteriorate this affects the quality of the film. The developing solution must be covered when not in use as it will be become oxidised by the air.

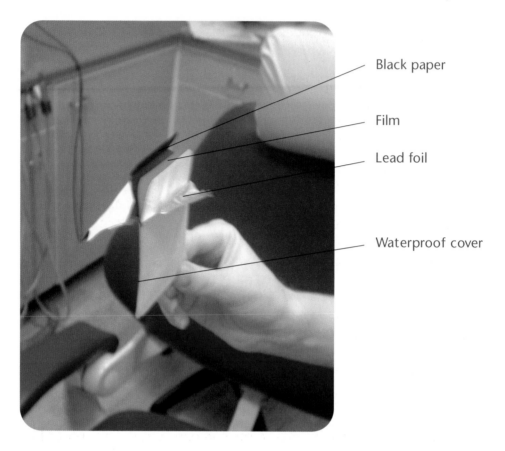

Black paper

Film

Lead foil

Waterproof cover

Fig. 7.6 An intraoral film that has been opened to show its different layers.

You must ensure that during the processing of dental radiographs you wear correct protective clothing to prevent any cross-infection and hazards from chemicals. Any chemical spillages should be cleaned immediately.

Automatic processing

This follows the same principle as manual processing but is done by a machine into which the film is loaded.

Digital processing

This involves no use of films or chemicals. The image is produced on a computer screen via the use of a sensor as the film.

Films should be stored in a cool, dark place away from direct heat and sunlight, and a check must be kept on the expiry dates. Ensure that stock is rotated, and use the oldest films first. Always ensure that there are plenty of films available so that you do not run out.

Chemicals must be stored upright in a cupboard away from heat and light. When changing chemicals you must always wear your personal protective clothing. Make sure that everyone knows that the developing machine will be out of use. Dispose of the used chemicals in the appropriate containers for waste collection. They must never be put down a sink or toilet. Each part of the machine must then be cleaned thoroughly to remove any excess chemicals and dried thoroughly. The developer and fixer and water are then put in their respective containers and, if using an automatic processor, all the rollers and the lid of the machine are put in place. Switch the power on the machine on to allow the chemicals to reach the correct temperature, then run a test film through to make sure that they are ready.

When viewing processed radiographs it is important that they are viewed in the correct way to ensure that an accurate diagnosis is made. Intraoral radiographs have a raised pimple in one corner. This should be facing you when viewing the radiograph. Extraoral radiographs should be fitted with a marker to indicate which is the left side and which is the right side. The morphology of the teeth will also help to indicate which way the radiographs should be viewed. Radiographs must be stored with the correct patient details and the date that they were taken.

See Table 7.1 for faults that can occur with radiographs.

Table 7.1 Faults that can occur while taking radiographs

FAULT	REASON FAULT OCCURRED
Blank film	Machine not switched on Film exposed on wrong side
Faint image	Out-of-date film Underdeveloped (developer too weak, too cold or exhausted)
Dark image	Overdeveloped (developer too strong, temperature too high or film left in too long)
Fogged image	Exposed to daylight before developing
Brown or green spots on film	Fixer process not complete Not in fixer long enough
White crystals on film	Film not washed thoroughly after fixing
Image of collimator on film (coning off)	Collimator tube not placed at correct angle during exposure
Blurred image	Patient or collimator has moved during exposure
Elongation or shortening of teeth on image	Incorrect angulation during exposure

Ionising radiation guidelines

There are important regulations that must be complied with when using ionising radiation.

The Ionising Radiation Regulations 1999 (IRR99)

These regulations are relevant to the protection of employees from ionising radiation in the workplace. The following guidelines have been issued:

- The Heath and Safety Executive must be informed of the use of X-rays and the introduction of any new equipment.

- A Radiation Protection Advisor and a Radiation Protection Supervisor must be appointed.

- Display local rules.

- Complete risk assessments (see Chapter 3).

- Have designated controlled areas.

- Have copies of all staff training records.

The Ionising Radiation (Medical Exposures) Regulations 2000 (IR (ME) R2000)

These are the guidelines that must be followed to ensure the restriction of the dosage of radiation to patients.

Radiation Protection Advisor

This is an organisation or person appointed to give advice on how to comply with IRR99. This organisation or person must be appointed in writing and can sometimes be whosoever provides the monitoring and servicing of the X-ray equipment.

Radiation Protection Supervisor

This is the person appointed in the practice who is responsible for making sure that all staff comply with IRR99 and that the guidelines set out in the local rules are followed. This is usually a dentist or qualified dental nurse who holds a certificate in dental radiography.

Local rules

These are to be displayed wherever any radiographs are taken and must show the following information:

- The name of the Radiation Protection Supervisor.

- The description of the controlled area. This is a 1.5 m radius around where the radiographs are taken. No one should be in the controlled area except for the person who is having the radiograph taken.

- Details of any contingency arrangements if there were any problems.
- Details of minimum exposure doses of radiation to staff and patients.

A radiation protection file should also be available, which contains all the above and other information such as:

- Details of staff training.
- Arrangements for pregnant staff.
- Details of risk assessment.
- Details of the arrangements for the maintenance and servicing of X-ray machines.
- Protocols for all working and processing procedures.

Only dentists and qualified dental nurses who have gained the postgraduate qualification in dental radiography for dental nurses are allowed to take radiographs.

Quality assurance

Quality assurance is important in radiography to ensure that good quality radiographs are always taken to enable an accurate diagnosis to be made, while at the same time making sure that radiation doses are kept as low as reasonably possible for staff and patients. This can be done by adhering to local rules at all times and ensuring that all staff are suitably trained. Test films should be run through processors or placed in the containers for manual developing at the beginning of a day. This is to ensure that the chemicals are suitable for processing. A record must be kept of each test radiograph and you must have a standard radiograph image quality to which you work.

8 Restorations

8: Restorations

Restorations are needed when a tooth has caries or the tooth has been fractured because of trauma. The size and position of the tooth and the individual concerned determine which filling material is used.

Reasons why teeth are restored

- To restore the function of the tooth to enable mastication (chewing).

- To restore the appearance (aesthetics) of the tooth.

- To restore the shape of the tooth to prevent food packing and plaque retention which would in turn prevent further problems such as caries occurring.

- To prevent more complex treatment being needed if broken teeth are left.

THE DENTAL NURSE'S ROLE IN RESTORATIVE PROCEDURES

Before the procedure

- It is the nurse's role before, during and after restorative procedures to make sure that the surgery is correctly prepared with the equipment and materials that will be needed during the procedure.

During the procedure

- Pass the required equipment to the dentist when needed.

- Aspirate throughout to remove water and debris so that the dentist has a clear field of vision and the patient remains comfortable.

- The aspirator can also be used to retract the cheek or lip to allow the tooth being worked on to be more visible. Alternatively, a mouth mirror may be used.

- Mix lining and filling materials correctly and in the appropriate amounts required.

- Ensure moisture control. Moisture control is very important during restorative procedures, not only for the comfort of the patient and to enable a clear field of vision for the dentist, but also because moisture can have an effect on some of the restorative materials used as they can be moisture sensitive and will not be successful if wet.

At the end of the procedure

- Ensure that all instruments are correctly cleaned and sterilised after use and the surgery cleaned adequately to prevent cross-infection.

Items of controlling moisture in the mouth

Items used to control the amount of moisture in the mouth and remove debris are:

- Aspirator
- Saliva ejector
- Cotton-wool roll
- Cotton pledget
- Rubber dam
- Dry Guards.

Equipment and materials used for restorative procedures

All dentists have their personal preferences regarding what equipment they use during a restoration. Here is a generic list of what should be made available by the dental nurse to the dentist for restorative procedures:

- Patient records
- Bib and glasses for patient
- Gloves, mask and glasses for dentist and nurse
- Mouth mirror
- Probe
- Tweezers
- Local anaesthetic cartridge, syringe and needle
- High-speed handpiece
- Contra-angle handpiece
- Burs
- 3-in-1 tip
- Aspirator tip
- Saliva ejector
- Mouthwash and tissues for patient

- Calcium hydroxide applicator
- Excavator
- Flat plastic
- Ward's carver
- Packer
- Burnisher
- Matrix band/strip
- Lining material
- Mixing pad and spatula.

See also Fig. 8.1.

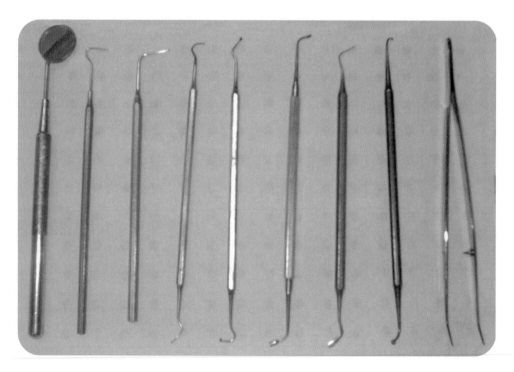

Fig. 8.1 A tray set up with instruments required for restorative procedures. From left to right: mouth mirror, probe, calcium hydroxide applicator, small excavator, large excavator, G. packer, Ward's carver, burnisher, College tweezers.

Restoration process

Before any tooth preparation is undertaken, the tooth or teeth to be prepared must be anaesthetised. To ensure that no pain or discomfort is felt while treating a vital tooth, ie a tooth that has a live and active blood supply, the tooth or teeth must be anaesthetised. The anaesthetic works by blocking the message to the brain that the pain is being felt. Local anaesthetics come in 2.2 ml cartridges and are used with a metal or disposable syringe and appropriate needle for injection (Figs 8.2–8.4).

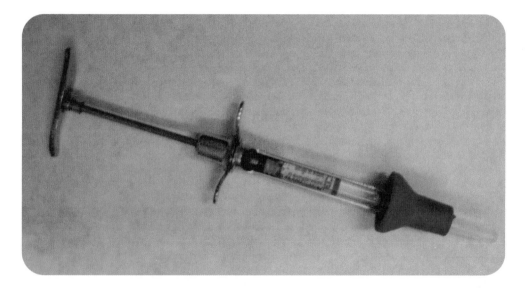

Fig. 8.2 Local anaesthetic syringe.

Usually an anaesthetic cartridge consists of the following constituents:

- Sterile water
- Vasoconstrictor (normally adrenaline epinephrine)
- Buffer salts
- Preservatives
- Anaesthetic solution.

A vasoconstrictor is used to narrow the blood vessels around the site of an injection to prolong the effect of anaesthesia. Adrenaline is the commonest vasoconstrictor but alternatives need to be available for people who have cardiac problems or high blood pressure because adrenaline increases the rate of blood flow around the body, eg felypressin. Four different techniques are used to administer local anaesthetics:

- Infiltration
- Nerve block
- Interaligamentary technique
- Intraosseous technique.

Infiltration (Fig. 8.3)

Infiltration can be given just around the gingivae immediately surrounding the tooth that need to be anaesthetised.

Nerve block (Fig. 8.4)

This technique anaesthetises a main nerve such as the inferior dental nerve and the mental nerve. This will enable anaesthesia for a whole group of teeth. For example, giving an inferior dental nerve block will anaesthetise all the teeth on one side of the mandible.

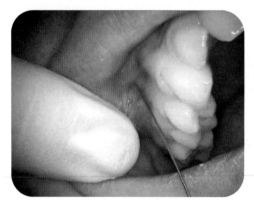

Fig. 8.3 Buccal infiltration.

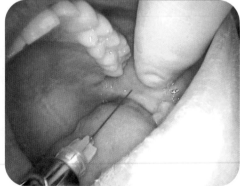

Fig. 8.4 Inferior dental nerve block.

Interligamentary technique

This can be used in conjunction with the above if adequate anaesthesia has not been successful. The anaesthetic solution is injected into the periodontal ligament around the tooth that needs to be anaesthetised. This will usually produce successful anaesthesia.

Intraosseous technique

This is when an injection is given directly into the alveolar bone to where the nerve supply runs. This produces successful anaesthesia instantly. A bur is first used to drill a hole into the bone, then a needle the same size as the bur is used to administer the local anaesthetic. When a tooth is being extracted, extra anaesthesia will need to be given around the palatal or the lingual nerve.

Cavity preparation

This is done to remove any caries from the cavity and prevent any further damage to the dentine or pulp, which would require more complex treatment. It is also meant to shape the cavity in such a way so that it retains the filling material.

Most cavity shaping is done using the high-speed handpiece. This handpiece can run at speeds of up to 500,000 rpm and the burs are held in place by friction. Water is essential during the use of this handpiece to keep the bur and tooth cool. The slow handpiece operates at a much slower speed and is used to remove soft dentine. Burs are held in a slow handpiece by the latch grip method. Following this, unsupported enamel is removed using the high-speed handpiece or excavators. Gingival margin trimmers and enamel chisels can also be used to remove unsupported enamel but are not commonly in use nowadays.

The size, position and shape of the cavity will determine whether a matrix band or strip will need to be used. A matrix band (Figs 8.5 and 8.6) is used to temporarily replace the missing wall in a Class II cavity. On anterior teeth, a matrix strip is used during composite or glass ionomer restorations to prevent the filling material from sticking to the adjacent teeth interproximally and also to help with the shape of the

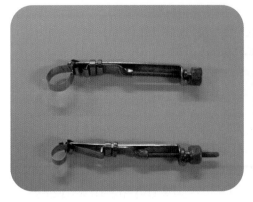

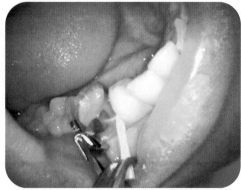

Fig. 8.5 Matrix bands ready for use.   Fig. 8.6 Matrix band in position.

restoration.

If the cavity is large, extra retention may be needed to hold the filling in place. This is done by the use of pins. These are inserted into the base of the cavity using the slow handpiece.

Types of restoration

Temporary restorations

These are named as such because they are only a temporary measure to keep a tooth comfortable before a permanent restoration is placed. Materials that can be used for temporary restorations are:

- Zinc oxide and eugenol
- Zinc phosphate
- Zinc polycarboxylate.

Glass ionomer can also be used though it is also used as a permanent filling material.

Zinc oxide and eugenol

This is provided as a powder (zinc oxide) and liquid (eugenol). It is mixed on a glass slab using a stainless steel spatula. This material can also be used as a sedative dressing, temporary cement and lining material.

Zinc phosphate

This is provided as zinc phosphate powder and phosphoric acid liquid. It is mixed on a cool glass slab with a stainless steel spatula. This material can also be used as a lining and a luting cement.

Zinc polycarboxylate

This is provided as a zinc oxide and polyacrylic acid powder with sterile water used as the liquid. It is mixed on a glass slab with a stainless steel spatula. This material can also be used as a lining or a luting cement.

When mixing any of these materials always check the manufacturer's instructions for the ratio of powder and liquid to be mixed.

Permanent restorations

These are named as such because they are used as permanent fillings in teeth.

Amalgam

Amalgam is the most commonly used filling material and is silver in colour. It is made by mixing an alloy containing copper, zinc, silver and tin with mercury. The required amount of alloy and the mercury can be pre-capsulated or the alloy powder and mercury liquid are placed into an amalgamator and the required amount is mixed. The materials are replenished when necessary. Capsulated amalgam is much safer as there is no direct contact with mercury.

Advantages:

- Cheap
- Easy to use
- Strong
- Long-lasting

Disadvantages:

- Mercury has toxic properties so handle with caution
- Appearance is not aesthetically pleasing
- Does not bond to tooth so more tooth needs to be removed to retain the filling in the cavity
- Constituents can irritate the pulp so a lining material is needed.

Composite

This is a tooth-coloured material composed of a resin and filler. The filler may consist of fine glass particles. To allow the composite to adhere to the tooth, the tooth must first be etched with 33% phosphoric acid. This is then rinsed to reveal a roughened surface to which the material can adhere to. A bonding agent is applied to the roughened surface and set using the curing light. This allows the composite to bond to the tooth. The composite is shaped and set again by the curing light. If using composite in large quantities, eg in a large posterior filling, the composite should be placed and set in small increments to ensure that all the filling is fully set.

Modern bonding agents now come as a one-step etch, primer and bonding agent.

Advantages:

- Tooth coloured and available in many shades
- Minimal tooth removal required as the material bonds to the tooth
- Sets immediately
- Metal free so does not irritate the pulp, minimal lining required.

Disadvantages:

- Not as strong
- Very moisture sensitive
- Longer to apply
- Curing lights needed which can cause damage to retina if the orange shields are not used correctly
- More expensive.

Glass ionomer

This comes as a powder of glass and polyacrylic acid and is mixed with sterile water on a waxed paper mixing pad with a metal spatula. Glass ionomer bonds directly to the tooth so there is no need for etch and bond. Once the glass ionomer has been placed and shaped, it will set and will need to be coated with a varnish to protect it from contamination from saliva while the setting process continues.

Advantages:

- Contains fluoride
- More aesthetically pleasing than amalgam
- Minimal tooth removal needed as bonds directly to tooth.

Disadvantages:

- Not very strong
- Takes a few hours to set fully so need protection from moisture
- Moisture sensitive
- Exact proportions to be used when mixing to ensure accurate setting, although nowadays glass ionomer is available in a capsulated form so there is no need to measure and the correct consistency will always be achieved.

Lining materials

These are placed before the permanent restoration at the base of the cavity, over the pulp chamber. A lining material is placed to protect the pulp from thermal and chemical shock.

The commonest lining material used is calcium hydroxide. This presents as two pastes: a base paste and a catalyst paste. Equal proportions of these are mixed to a uniform colour on a waxed paper pad with a stainless steel spatula.

If a cavity is deep a sublining may be used on top of the calcium hydroxide to provide a denser barrier and increased protection for the pulp chamber. For this sublining the materials mentioned previously such as polycarboxylate and glass ionomer can be used.

9 Fostering People's Equality, Diversity and Rights

9: Fostering People's Equality, Diversity and Rights

This chapter looks at how the dental nurse can work in ways that recognise the rights of the patients, enabling them to be treated equally and valuing them as individuals. The dental nurse needs to be aware of patients' rights and support patients where necessary in exercising these rights. At all times the dental nurse must maintain patient confidentiality, working within statutory and organisational frameworks and procedures. The dental nurse therefore needs to work in ways that promote:

- People's rights and responsibilities
- Equality and diversity of patients
- Patients' rights with regard to the confidentiality of their information.

To enable dental nurses to fulfil their duties when fostering the equality, diversity and rights of all patients within their care, they first need to identify and understand:

- Ethnic groups
- Religious denominations
- Social backgrounds.

They also need to have information regarding their patients' disabilities and medical history.

Ethnic groups and religious denominations

When considering ethnic groups in our society we need to think of differences in culture, dress, diet, language and religion within each group of people.

People with learning difficulties

People with learning difficulties can often function independently or with support from carers or family members within the community. Tasks or instructions given should be appropriate to their level of understanding and skills.

People with physical disabilities

Many patients treated in the dental surgery suffer from physical disabilities, you must be sensitive to any special requirements in care they may require.

Patients with medical problems

A patient's medical history and present medical condition must always be fully disclosed to the dental team. This information must be updated and discussed at regular intervals. A patient's medical condition forms a very important part of treatment planning, drugs and medicaments to be administered, and the timing of their dental appointments.

What is discrimination?

Discrimination against people can occur in our society today because of religious beliefs, culture, sexual orientation, disabilities or race. It can result in a lack of career opportunity, exclusion from social groups, poor education opportunities and limited access to services. Discrimination can take the form of verbal abuse and even physical attacks. It is often a result of ignorance, lack of understanding or information, and sometimes even fear.

Recognising your own prejudices

One of the hardest things to acknowledge can be your own prejudices and how they can affect what you do. Prejudices are often a result of our own personal beliefs, values and attributes. Everyone has their own beliefs and values, but at all times you must be aware of them and how they can affect your day-to-day life and work.

Think about the basic principles that apply to you in your own life. For example, you may have a belief that you should always be honest, so think about what that could mean for the way you work – you could find it difficult to work alongside and be pleasant to someone who you found out had lied extensively.

Once you are aware of your own beliefs and values, and have recognised how important they are, you must think about how to accept the beliefs and values of others. The individuals with whom you work are all different, as are the patients whom you treat, and so it is important to recognise and accept that diversity.

Reducing the impact of discrimination

How can you, as an employee, evaluate your role as a dental nurse faster and encourage equality by treating everyone the same, while acknowledging that diversity exists as all people are different? Think about the steps that you can take to reduce discrimination:

- Try to avoid language that could be deemed racist and could cause offence to others.

- Try not to use words that may distress or degrade people with problems or disabilities.

- Support patients suitably in challenging any barriers that may exist, eg, entrance to the dental practice, access to the dental surgery.

- Refuse to accept behaviour that you recognise as discrimination.

- If you are uncertain what to do in a particular situation, discuss the problem with your superiors.

- Try to assist people with specific impairments.

- Try to develop a greater understanding of the views and preferences of disabled patients in your own dental practice.

Fostering people's rights and responsibilities

To look at rights in terms of how they affect the people with whom you work and the patients for whom you care, this section discusses the various Acts that have been developed to protect various groups of people within society.

Race Relations Act 1976

This Act prohibits all forms of racial discrimination relating to employment, housing and services. It also makes it an offence to encourage racial hatred. The Act covers all discriminations, including colour, nationality and race.

Sex Discrimination Act 1975

This Act was put into place to ensure equal rights for men and women in respect of employment, goods, services and facilities. It prevents discrimination against women in employment. The equal opportunities commission supporting the working of the law oversees the Act. The Equal Pay Act 1970 provides a woman the right to be employed on the same terms and conditions as a man, while being employed in the same type of work.

Disability Discrimination Act 1995

This Act was developed to provide rights for people with disabilities with regard to obtaining access to employment, education, transport and housing. Under this Act employers must not treat a disabled person less favourably in the workplace than an able-bodied person. The employer must examine any changes that need to be made to make the workplace more accessible and facilities more desirable, making it more possible for a disabled person to secure a job.

Access for disabled people to education and transport means that both schools and colleges need to produce details of how a student will be able to access courses, regardless of their disabilities. In recent times taxis, coaches and buses have been designed to allow easy access for those people who have mobility problems or are wheelchair bound.

Shops, restaurants and all those who provide a service, including dental practices, now have to ensure that disabled people are able to make use of the service. Landlords are not allowed to discriminate against anyone with a disability when letting a property and are not allowed to charge higher rents than would be charged to able-bodied people.

Children's Act 1989

This Act provides children the right to be protected from 'significant harm'. This identifies parental responsibility first, then parental rights, so ensuring that children are not treated as property over which rights can be exercised. It also ensures that such places as children's nurseries or residential establishments are regularly inspected, ensuring that certain standards are maintained.

Rights under charters, guidelines and policies

Rights are designed to improve the services that people receive. The Patient's Charter clearly sets out the service that people can expect from the National Health Service. Despite not being an Act of Parliament, the Patient's Charter is effective because it has the backing of the government and all NHS trusts are obliged to work towards the charter.

The key role of charters is to make the expected standards public. If people know what they have the right to expect from the health service then they can take steps to complain and have things put right if these standards are not met.

Maintaining confidentiality of information

What is confidentiality?

An important requirement of anyone working as a member of the dental team is at all times to be trustworthy. Working as a dental nurse you will need to make confidentiality a part of your life.

Confidentiality means not giving any information about a patient to anyone unless there is a valid reason to do so. In your role as a dental nurse you will be expected to maintain confidentiality in respect of each patient's personal details and medical conditions. Great care should be taken when handling sensitive information.

HOW CAN THE DENTAL NURSE HELP MAINTAIN PATIENT CONFIDENTIALITY?

- Any information either disclosed to you by a patient or recorded on a patient's notes should not be given to any other source unless you have been told to do so.

- You should not discuss patients outside the working environment.

- Any conversations that you have with a patient about personal issues should be done in a private area of the practice or away from public areas such as the waiting room or reception area.

- All written records should be stored safely and securely, and should be given only to members of staff within the practice. All patient records held on a computer system are protected by the Data Protection Act 1984 and should be protected by appropriate practice security procedures.

What happens when a patient wants to complain?

The General Dental Council requests that all dental practices adopt a practice procedure to deal with any complaints from patients or their relatives. At any time during or after their dental treatment a patient has the right to complain about the treatment that they have received or the attitudes of the staff, or if they feel that they have been discriminated against for any reason.

All complaints should be swiftly dealt with to reach a resolution. It is therefore very important that all members of the dental team are aware of the correct practice procedure when handling any complaints. The patients within the practice also need to be aware of the correct method of lodging a complaint. At all times the practice procedure needs to be methodically followed. All complaints should be resolved at the earliest opportunity. In more serious cases, patients may want to complain to the General Dental Council, which will review the complaint and decide if serious professional misconduct has taken place and then act accordingly.

10 Communication

10: Communication

It is important for all members of the dental team to be able to understand how to communicate with people, even when difficulties or barriers to communication may exist. Communication is not just about talking to people – where barriers do not exist, it is also about being able to make suitable contact with those people who, for whatever reason, find communication much harder.

What is communication?

Communication is the exchange of information from one person to another by a combination of the following methods:

- Speaking
- Eye contact or facial expression
- Body language
- Writing down information for the other person to read
- Showing them a series of pictures, drawings or diagrams
- Body positioning
- Hand signing.

To make communication effective the dental nurse needs also to ensure that the environment is suitably prepared, and that the method of communication used is suitable for the particular patient.

Determining the nature and scope of the communication problems and differences

Before you – as a dental nurse – can communicate effectively with the patient, you need to establish what communication differences exist.

People who do not speak English

Patients who do not speak English can often feel isolated and frustrated when they cannot understand you and you cannot understand them. Patients can become frightened when they do not understand what you are doing to them. They may also feel excluded and unimportant when the nurse is communicating with the dentist.

ABCDEFG
HISKHLM
NOPQRST

Cultural differences

Culture is about more than the spoken word. It is about the way a person lives, thinks and relates to others. For example, in some cultures women are not allowed to speak to men whom they do not know.

Learning difficulties

The degree of disability of the patient may limit their ability to understand what you are explaining to them and reply to you suitably. It is also likely that patients with a short attention span will need to have information repeated to them again and again.

Hearing impairment

As communication is a two-way process, it is difficult for a patient who has partial hearing or no hearing to understand what the dental nurse is saying to them. Even patients who wear a hearing aid may have only limited hearing that can often be muffled and indistinct. Patients may therefore become withdrawn. Background noise mixed together with sounds of voices can often make it very difficult for the patient to pick out the sound of the voice of the person who is speaking to them. A patient with hearing problems often has problems with speaking and making themselves understood to others. This can result in the patient becoming frustrated and angry.

Visual impairment

Visual impairment can cause many communication problems. Not only is the patient unable to pick up visual signals that are being given out by someone who is speaking but, because the patient is unaware of these signals, the person may also fail to give appropriate signals in communication. Consequently, as the patient cannot see your facial expression or body language, they may misinterpret information being given to them.

Establishing communication when problems exist

For dental nurses to be able to communicate effectively with the patient they must first be able to establish if any communication problems are evident. How can you do this?

- Look at and read the patient's notes/records. Have any communication problems been recorded previously? If so, what are they? Have any successful methods of communication been suggested?

- When meeting the patient are there any physical characteristics that may indicate communication problems, such as the patient present wearing a hearing aid.

- When speaking to the patient, do they understand what you are saying? Do they give adequate answers, or do they appear puzzled or unclear about what you are saying to them? Do they hesitate to reply or not acknowledge you at all?

- Does the patient indicate that they do not understand or speak English?

- How do nervous or frightened patients react when you speak to them? Are they focusing more on their fear than on what is being said?

- Is the environment that you are in making communication more difficult? Is there loud background noise? Do you have to speak loudly to be understood? A busy dental surgery can often be a very noisy place.

Dealing with barriers to communication

For dental nurses to communicate effectively with their patients, it is essential that wherever possible they are able to overcome any barriers that may exist.

Patients with language barriers

As we live in a multicultural society, English may not be the first language of many patients who attend the practice. It may be necessary for alternative methods to be used in overcoming language barriers, such as using interpreters. Many health authorities are now able to offer the services of an interpreter. This service enables the dental practice to either pre-book an interpreter to attend the practice and directly interact between the dental team and patient, or to converse over the telephone with the patient. Alternatively, ask a member of the patient's family who can speak and understand English to attend with the patient for each appointment.

Patients with hearing problems

Many patients with hearing problems wear hearing aids. Background noise can hinder the efficiency of a hearing aid, making it less efficient. It is therefore important that wherever possible the amount of background noise is minimised by switching off the aspirator or any music, and that you speak to patients away from the noise of the reception or waiting room.

Patients with hearing problems may be able to lipread. If you have established the fact that a patient can lipread it is important that you position yourself in front of the patient so that they can see your face and mouth. Always remember to remove your facemask before speaking.

Use body language and facial expression to reinforce your communication with the patient. Hand signing may also be an appropriate way of communicating with the patient as long as you have the skills and experience, and the patient understands sign language. Writing down instructions or supplying the patient with leaflets or instruction sheets can also enable the patient to understand the message that you are trying to put across.

Patients with visual problems

It is essential that you always keep the patient informed of what is going to happen and what you are doing, so that they are not suddenly surprised or feel uncomfortable and fearful about the treatment being carried out.

Speak directly to the patient so that your voice does not 'trail away' if you move around the surgery. Ensure that the patient is guided if necessary around the reception, waiting area and surgery, eliminating the likelihood of accidents or injuries. If possible, have instruction sheets and practice leaflets written in Braille to assist the patient.

Patients who are frightened or worried about receiving dental treatment

Often when patients are frightened of their dental treatment it can have a detrimental effect on their communication with the dentist or nurse, or on listening to what is being said to them. It is therefore important for the dental nurse wherever possible to relieve the patient's anxiety. Speak clearly and calmly to the patient, reassure them and give the patient suitable time to speak, explain their fears and ask questions without interrupting them.

Always allow the patient time to get accustomed to the surgery environment. Allow time for patients to make themselves comfortable, allowing them to become more relaxed. Make sure that patients are kept informed of what is going to happen, and answer their questions honestly. Patients who become upset because they are frightened may also become embarrassed. It is important to reassure them to alleviate their embarrassment.

Patients with learning difficulties

It is important that all patients understand any instructions or any explanations that you give them. The nurse must ensure that patients with learning difficulties also understand what is being said to them by speaking clearly, using simple language that they can understand. The help of a third party, a family member or carer, can be useful as they can speak to the patient to explain what is being said to them. Pictures can be used to get the message across sufficiently, and reassuring the patient before, during and after treatment can have a beneficial effect on the patient – enabling them to feel more confident and comfortable about what is happening to them.

REFLECTING ON YOUR PRACTICE

It is important for you as a dental nurse to reflect on how you have contributed to effective communication with a patient where barriers exist:

- Think about the particular barrier: how did it affect communication between you and the patient?

- What methods did you adopt to overcome these barriers?

- Did your methods work or could you have used other methods with a better result?

Always remember to write notes on the patient records to inform other members of staff within the practice of a patient's communication difficulties, and what methods you have used to remove or overcome these problems.

11 Fixed Prostheses

11: Fixed Prostheses

A fixed prosthesis is a prosthesis that cannot be removed, eg a crown, bridge, veneer or inlay.

Crowns

A crown is a false tooth placed over an existing tooth to restore function or appearance. A crown may be needed:

- if a tooth is heavily restored
- if a tooth is root filled, which will therefore be more brittle
- to correct malalignments
- if a change in appearance is required.

There are many different types of crown.

Gold crowns – These are made from a gold alloy which is very strong.

Bonded crowns (Fig. 11.1) – These are made from a metal substructure, which is coated with a tooth-coloured porcelain to give them a more natural appearance.

All porcelain or ceramic crowns – These are made without any metal and give a more natural appearance to the crown.

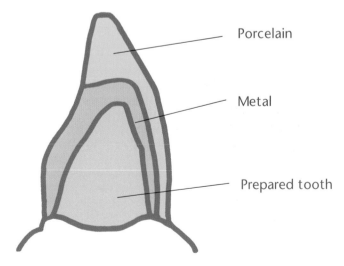

Porcelain

Metal

Prepared tooth

Fig. 11.1 Cross-section of a porcelain-bonded crown on an anterior tooth.

Post crown – If a tooth has been root treated then the tooth will be much weaker than a vital tooth, so a post crown will be required. For this a post is placed inside the root to give it strength and then the crown is placed on top of the post.

Which type of crown is used depends on the level of appearance or strength required, or sometimes the patient's personal preference.

Bridges

A bridge is used to fill a gap in the mouth where a tooth or teeth may be missing. They are made when a removable prosthesis is not possible or cannot be tolerated by the patient. The advantages of a bridge are:

- they can look and feel much better in the mouth than a denture
- they are healthier for the mouth
- they are ideal for patients who suffer from a bad gag reflex, as the bridge does not cover the palate.

The missing teeth are known as pontics and the teeth that retain the bridge are known as abutments or retainers. There are different types of bridge that can be made.

Maryland/adhesive bridge

This is composed of a single pontic with metal wings (Fig. 11.2) that are attached to one or both sides of the pontic. The advantage of this type of bridge is that it requires minimal tooth preparation.

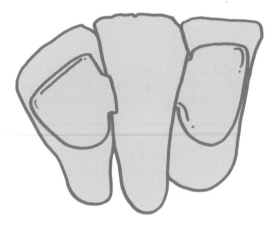

Fig. 11.2 Fixed bridge – Maryland type.

Fixed–fixed bridge

This is composed of one or more pontics with the teeth on either side of the gap retaining the bridge in place (Fig. 11.3).

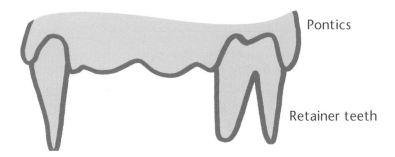

Fig. 11.3 A fixed/fixed bridge replacing a missing premolar and molar.

Cantilever bridge

This consists usually of one pontic with only one of the adjacent teeth being used as a retainer (Fig. 11.4). A spring cantilever bridge can also be made where the retainer is not next to the pontic, but a metal bar attached to the bridge goes around the lingual or palatal surface to attach to the retainer in a different part of the arch.

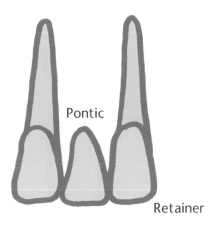

Fig. 11.4 A cantilever bridge for missing lateral incisor.

Movable bridge

A movable joint (Fig. 11.5) may be made between a pontic and a retainer to make the bridge more flexible. As with bonded crowns these bridges are made of a metal substructure, coated with tooth-coloured porcelain.

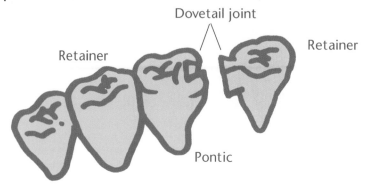

Dovetail joint

Retainer

Retainer

Pontic

Fig. 11.5 A movable bridge. Note the 'dovetail' joint (arrowed) between the pontic and one of the retainers. This allows slight flexibility.

Veneers

A veneer (Fig. 11.6) is a very thin piece of tooth-coloured porcelain used to cover the front surface of a tooth to change its appearance, colour, shape or position. The advantage of a veneer is that minimal tooth preparation is required.

Indications of veneers:

- Discoloured teeth
- Peg laterals
- Malaligned teeth
- Rotated teeth
- Midline diastemas.

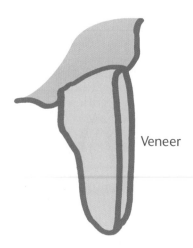

Veneer

Fig. 11.6 A veneer restoration. A thin section of the labial surface of the tooth has been removed and replaced by a veneer.

Inlays

An inlay (Fig. 11.7) is a filling that is constructed in the dental laboratory rather than a filling which is placed directly in the mouth in the surgery. Inlays can be made of a gold alloy, composite or porcelain. An inlay is preferred to a direct filling when a strong restoration is required. The advantage of an inlay over a crown is that minimal tooth preparation is required.

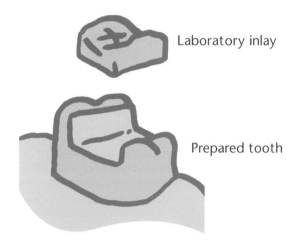

Laboratory inlay

Prepared tooth

Fig. 11.7 An inlay.

THE DENTAL NURSE'S ROLE IN FIXED PROSTHESIS TREATMENT

For each of the fixed prostheses the procedure follows exactly the same stages and the instruments and equipment required for each are also similar.

- It is the nurse's duty to ensure that all equipment and materials needed are made available for the dentist to use when required.

- Sterilisation and cross-infection procedures must be followed.

- Aspiration and retraction of soft tissues when required and monitoring the patient and the procedure throughout.

Preparation stage

The instruments and equipment that are needed for the preparation stage are similar for all types of fixed prosthesis:

- Patient records
- Mouth mirror
- Probe
- Tweezers
- Local anaesthetic cartridge, needle and syringe
- High-speed handpiece
- Selection of crown prep burs
- 3-in-1 tip
- Aspirator tip
- Saliva ejector
- Cotton-wool rolls
- Bib and safety glasses
- Mouthwash and tissues
- Laboratory prescription and laboratory bag
- Disinfectant solution for impressions
- Alginate, bowl, spatula, measuring scoops
- Polyether- or addition-cured silicone impression material
- Impression trays and fixative
- Shade guide
- Temporary crown material
- Retraction cord
- Astringent
- Pink sheet wax
- Flat plastic instrument.

This is a generic selection of equipment and materials for this procedure. As with restorations each dentist has their own personal preference for instruments and materials that they like to use.

Once the surgery has been prepared for the procedure the patient can be brought into the surgery and given bib and glasses to use as protection. The tooth/teeth to be prepared are anaesthetised. Upper and lower impressions are then taken with alginate, of which study models will be made. These will show how the patient bites together and the impressions can also be used to make temporary crowns. These are usually taken only during crown and bridge preparation.

Preliminary impression taking

Alginate is the most common of the impression materials as it is used for a wide variety of purposes:

- study models
- constructing dentures and special trays
- to make temporary crowns
- constructing orthodontic appliances.

Alginate is an irreversible hydrocolloid. It is mixed with tepid water at a ratio of powder/liquid as recommended in the manufacturer's instructions. Tepid water is used because if the water is too hot the alginate will set too fast, and if the water is too cold it will set too slowly. All alginates are supplied with measures for the water and the powder. It is then thoroughly mixed together, vigorously to avoid any air bubbles, and produces a stiff, uniform mix. Air bubbles need to be avoided as these affect the accuracy of the impression.

The impression material is then loaded into an impression tray which should have been pre-treated with adhesive to prevent the impression coming away from the tray when removing it from the mouth after the alginate has set. Once it is removed from the mouth the impression should be rinsed under running water and placed in dilute hypochlorite solution for approximately 20 minutes.

Preparation of the tooth

The tooth or teeth are then prepared using the high-speed handpiece and appropriate burs. It is the dental nurse's role to aspirate water and debris and retract the soft tissues when necessary. For all crowns, except a post crown, the tooth is prepared by reducing the dimensions of the tooth all the way around and also the height.

For a post crown the inside of the root of the tooth is prepared using Gates/Glidden drills (Fig. 11.10) and the preferred post kit to shape the inside of the root canal and remove some of the old root filling. It is important to make the post as long as practically possible to improve retention. A crown is then made to fit over the top of the post.

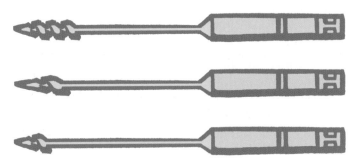

Fig. 11.8 Gates/Glidden drills.

For all bridges, except for adhesive/Maryland bridges, the teeth are prepared in the same way as for most crowns by reducing the dimensions all around and the height. For an adhesive bridge a small amount of the palatal or lingual surface of the adjacent teeth is removed. When preparing veneers a small amount of the front surface of the tooth is removed. Preparation for an inlay is similar to that for a filling but the sides of the preparation must be parallel, with no undercuts.

During any preparation the gingival tissue can sometimes become traumatised and bleed. Astringent can be used to stop this bleeding. Sometimes before the impression is taken, a retraction cord can be placed around the gingival margin for crowns, bridges or veneers to make the margins of the preparation much clearer to see, especially if they are below the level of the gingivae.

Final impression taking

An impression is taken of the tooth or teeth that have been prepared using either an addition, cured silicone or polyether material. This material is used as it is much more accurate than alginate. When mixing this type of material you need to be aware that some types of gloves can affect the correct setting of the material. Also the disinfectant process can distort some of these impression materials so it is important to check the manufacturer's instructions. Once the impression has set it must be removed carefully from the mouth, rinsed under running water and disinfected accordingly.

Temporisation

Temporary crowns and bridges (but not adhesive bridges) are made from a cold cure acrylic material that is tooth-coloured.

They can be made by using the original alginate impression taken at the start of the procedure. The temporary material is prepared in the impression and then placed over the tooth until set. This will then make a temporary of the original tooth. Ready-made crown forms can also be used which can be tooth-coloured and are available in various sizes and trimmed where necessary. Metal crowns are available that can be used on posterior teeth.

Temporary crowns and bridges are cemented in place with a zinc oxide and eugenol-based cement so that it can be easily removed when the permanent crown is ready to fit.

For veneers and inlay preparations it is usually sufficient to cover the area with a temporary filling material to prevent sensitivity or food packing.

Why are temporaries made?

A temporary prosthesis is made for the following reasons:

- To hold a space between teeth
- To prevent sensitivity
- To prevent gingival overgrowth
- To prevent over-eruption
- To prevent food packing
- For appearance.

The laboratory prescription is then written up with details for the dental technician about the type of prosthesis that they should construct. If the prosthesis is to be tooth coloured a shade is chosen and noted on the laboratory prescription. Also on the prescription you must write the patient's name, dentist's name and the date that the dentist requires the work back. Usually arrangements will be in place with the laboratory that the practice uses as to how long they need to construct the prosthesis.

Laboratory stage

The prosthesis is then made in the laboratory as directed by the prescription. It is important to build a good relationship with the dental technicians whom the practice uses, so that they produce a high standard of work for you and help you out with any problems that you may have. It is not uncommon for a technician to come to the dental surgery to help a dentist choose a shade for a complex case or even to construct something in less time for you out of good faith.

Insertion stage

The instruments required are:

- Mouth mirror
- Probe
- Tweezers
- Local anaesthetic cartridge, needle and syringe
- Lab work
- High-speed handpiece and burs
- 3-in-1 tip
- Ward's carver
- Articulating paper and forceps
- Cement, spatula and mixing pad
- Floss
- Mouthwash
- Tissues

- Aspirator tip
- Saliva ejector
- Bib
- Glasses
- Hand mirror.

First of all the temporary is removed. Local anaesthetic may or may not be required. Once the temporary has been taken out any debris is removed from around the area and the permanent prosthesis can be placed. The prosthesis should be shown to the patient before it is cemented so that they are happy with the appearance.

The majority of crowns, bridges and inlays can be cemented using zinc phosphate, zinc polycarboxylate or glass ionomer cement (see Chapter 8). Adhesive bridges, veneers and some types of crowns or inlays are cemented using a type of bonding system that involves etch, bond and a resin-based material (see Chapter 8). Once the prosthesis has been cemented, any excess cement is removed and the bite checked with articulating paper.

12 Removable Prostheses

12: Removable Prostheses

Removable dentures are constructed when there are teeth missing and the patient has chosen a denture as opposed to a fixed prosthesis (crowns, bridges or implants – see Chapters 11 and 16). Dentures are used to replace missing teeth, to maintain the function of mastication (chewing), for aesthetics and to keep any remaining teeth in their correct position.

When all the teeth are missing, this is called being 'edentulous'. When missing teeth are not replaced, and the opposing teeth are still present, they can over-erupt due to their lack of function. Adjacent teeth can also tilt into the space where the tooth/teeth used to be, as the surrounding structures are lost. Bone loss will also gradually occur, as, without the tooth, the surrounding bone becomes redundant and will resorb to a lower level. When there are several teeth missing, particularly the anterior teeth, then, as the bone resorbs, the shape of the patient's face will alter, and also lose height. Dentures can replace the lost support along with replacement teeth to return a satisfactory appearance.

There are different types of removable denture:

- Chrome cobalt (metal)
- Acrylic (plastic)
- Immediate dentures.

For partial dentures, there are two main choices – acrylic or chrome cobalt. As the name suggests, there are two different types of metal involved in the latter – chrome and cobalt. This particular type of denture has been around since 1955, and is often a more comfortable choice, as the skeleton framework covers less of the mucosa than an acrylic denture, and it is far stronger.

Advantages:
- Less chance of food and plaque trapping
- Oxygen can access the mucosa more easily than under an acrylic denture. This helps prevent conditions such as denture sore mouth.

Disadvantages:

- They can take longer to make (due to the metal being difficult to adjust compared with acrylic)
- More expensive.

Acrylic dentures are made out of a mixture of a polymer powder and a monomer liquid. The two are mixed into a dough-type mixture in the dental laboratory. They can be either chemically cured by a catalyst in the liquid, (cold curing) or by heating in a special oven (heat curing). The former type of curing acrylic (cold cure acrylic) is often used when relining dentures. Poorly fitting dentures can cause ulceration of the mucosa, and hence dentures need to be regularly checked by the dentist, because even the health status of an edentulous mouth can change.

Before making acrylic or chrome cobalt dentures, the patient's full medical and dental history will be taken by the dentist. During this appointment, the dentist may take radiographs to determine the health of the remaining teeth, the level of the bone and health of the joints.

The height of the face will be taken with a Willis bite gauge. A particular problem that can occur when the patient loses face height, is angular cheilitis, which is a combined streptococcal/staphylococcal and candida infection that occurs as the folds in the facial skin become moist and prone to infection. The signs of this condition are red and cracked corners of the mouth, often with a sore crust. After taking a swab, this is treated with miconazole cream, which will act on all three sources of infection. It should not be assumed that the patient's condition is caused by loss of facial height, as other underlying medical problems, such as anaemia, can also cause this, hence the importance of a complete updated medical history.

An impression is then taken and the dental nurse should rinse the impression to remove any blood and debris, disinfecting this immediately. You must, as with all dirty instruments when infection is present, place the impression in a disinfectant bath (sodium hypochlorite) according to the manufacturer's instructions. Once it is sent to the laboratory, the laboratory technician will pour plaster of Paris into the impression mould and, from this, form a model of the patient's mouth, so that the denture can be constructed.

Acrylic and chrome cobalt dentures are constructed in several stages (Table 12.1) and these are described below.

Table 12.1 Stages of construction of partial dentures

STAGE	MATERIALS REQUIRED AND REASON
First stage	
Alginate impression	Alginate/mixing bowl/spatula
Wax bite	Shade guide Sheet wax (Fig. 12.1)
Second stage	
Special tray impression	Special tray/alginate/mixing bowl
Third stage	
Try in (can also be second try-in stage)	Denture either made in wax or prepared in metal finish if set as chrome cobalt. Maybe returned from laboratory on an anatomical articulator
Correct height of occlusal rims	Wax knife/Bunsen burner/Lecron carver/acrylic baseplates/Willis bite gauge (to confirm correct facial height)
Face bow registration	This can also be used in conjunction with the articulator, to record the position of the upper occlusal rim in relation to the mandibular condyles
Fourth stage	
Fitting the denture	Denture is finally fitted Can also be adjusted with straight handpiece and burs Occlusion can be tested by using articulating paper and occlusal indicator wax, and adjusted with a straight handpiece and appropriate burs Face mirror Aftercare instructions for patient

Impression trays

There are two different types of impression tray (Fig. 12.2) to choose from: edentulous and partial. Edentulous trays have a shorter depth to fit over the alveolar ridge, and the partial tray is deeper and fits over any remaining teeth. The trays come in a variety of sizes to accommodate different patients' mouths. They can be made of metal or plastic, and come as either perforated or non-perforated, to accommodate the material used and the preference of the dentist.

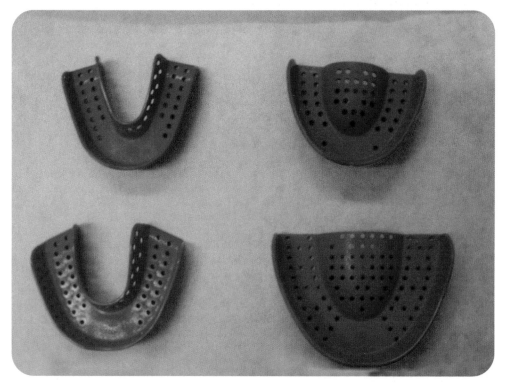

Fig. 12.2 Impression trays.

Special trays

A special tray is constructed from an alginate impression, for taking a more accurate final impression. The special tray is formed from a shellac or an acrylic baseplate.

Alginate impression material is prepared by mixing a measured dose of powder with a measured dose of water. It is mixed together into a smooth paste. This is mixed thoroughly and quickly, and then placed into a perforated impression tray (which should have been tried in the patient's mouth beforehand for size).

THE DENTAL NURSE'S ROLE DURING IMPRESSION TAKING

While the impression is setting in the patient's mouth, you may need to offer support and reassurance to the patient, as, particularly with upper trays, some susceptible patients can gag with this procedure. You will need to encourage the patient to breathe steadily through their nose rather than their mouth, as this will ease their gag reflex and allow them to concentrate on their breathing instead. It would also be handy to have a kidney dish ready though, just in case!

Advantages of alginate:

- Elastic material
- Sets quickly
- Relatively economical to use.

The disadvantage of alginate is that distortion can occur if not kept moist by wrapping in a moist cloth and casting quickly. The wrapped impression can be kept overnight in a refrigerator if required.

Immediate dentures

Immediate dentures are fitted immediately after extractions. This is so that the patient's function and aesthetics are restored without delay. There will therefore be two sets of aftercare instructions to give – extraction aftercare and denture aftercare.

Extraction aftercare

- No rinsing for the next 24 hours – if the patient does so the blood clot may be washed away and cause a painful dry socket.

- After this time, rinse with one teaspoon of salt in a tumbler of warm water.

- Take paracetamol before the local anaesthetic wears off, and thereafter if there is any further discomfort or pain. Follow the instructions on the package insert. **Do not take** aspirin, as this thins the blood and may cause unnecessary bleeding.

- There may be some remaining blood in the mouth following extraction, and this can get mixed with saliva. However, if any bleeding does occur, bite firmly on the packs given for about 10 minutes until the bleeding stops.

- If there is severe pain or bleeding, contact the surgery immediately.

Denture aftercare (immediate dentures)

- Remove the denture after 24 hours, and wash thoroughly using a clean toothbrush, or new soft nailbrush and warm soapy water. (Keep this separate from other nailbrushes.)

- Remove after eating to clean and also remove morning and night.

- If the dentist has advised, the denture can be worn while sleeping; otherwise remove at night and leave in cool water after cleaning.

- If there are any sore spots or painful areas beneath the denture, contact the surgery to arrange an appointment.

- Keep the next appointment. It is normal for the denture to require adjustments over the following few months, as the bone level will be changing to a different and lower height, now that the natural teeth are gone, and the denture may require relining.

Relining dentures

Relining is required some time after the construction of a denture. This is because of bone shrinkage around the alveolar ridge after a tooth/teeth have been extracted, as discussed above. As the denture may have been made only a few months previously, it would not require remaking completely.

An impression paste, such as zinc oxide relining paste, can be used and the denture can then be adjusted in the laboratory, or a clear soft gel relining material can also be mixed by the dental nurse and applied by the dentist, and worn immediately by the patient afterwards. The soft gel lining can also be used to cushion sore areas on the mucosa.

The advantage of denture relining material is that it will improve the fit of the denture immediately afterwards. The disadvantages of zinc oxide relining paste are that undercuts within the denture are not reproduced, and the patient may have to be without their denture for a short time afterwards. A soft gel relining material can wear, but this can be redone at a later stage.

Impression compound

Also called composition, this material is heated and softened from a solid slab or stick and used to take an accurate impression. The sticks are coloured green, brown or red. Care must be taken not to overheat before placing in the patient's mouth, to avoid burning the mucosa. The compound is used to add height and depth to a special tray, by placing it around the periphery of the tray, or as a baseplate. This makes the peripheral seal and impression more accurate.

The advantage of composition material is that it is does not require mixing. The disadvantages are that it is easily distorted when being removed from an undercut area and requires heating to enable it to become malleable.

Over-dentures

An over-denture can be constructed when there are roots that remain intact and healthy, and the patient's alveolar ridge may be at risk of becoming so low that denture retention would be extremely difficult. The roots will have to be root treated and contoured to provide a satisfactory foundation for the over-denture.

Cleidocranial dysostosis

Cleidocranial dysostosis is a congenital deformity in which over-dentures are invaluable. Bone formation and development of the teeth are affected. The patient has short stature, and there is delayed closure of the fontanelle in the skull. The mandible protrudes as does the brow bone (frontal bossing). The nasal bridge is wide causing the eyes to be wider apart (hypertelorism), and there is scoliosis of the spine. The person often has the ability to bring and touch their shoulders together as the clavicle is malformed and/or missing. They can have hearing difficulties and also be prone to multiple ear infections.

As far as the dental condition goes, the natural shedding of the deciduous teeth is delayed, and they do not often shed naturally. The permanent teeth are often slow in erupting, and may not erupt or even be present, and the roots of the teeth may also be malformed. An over-denture in this case is invaluable, as the permanent teeth may simply not erupt to allow full function and satisfactory appearance.

Obturators

Obturators are used when part of the palate is missing. An impression of the palate is taken when the child is born in order to construct an obturator to allow normal feeding to take place. The obturator contains a 'plug' to seal the cavity within the palate. As the child grows, so the size of the obturator has to change, until surgery is done to close the hole, with bone grafts. Cleft palates often have associated cleft (or 'hair') lip defects, unilateral or bilateral. These are also corrected with enormous success by surgery carried out by an oral surgeon. Following cleft palate and cleft lip surgery (carried out in a series of operations throughout the child's growing life), orthodontic treatment is also performed to correct the associated malocclusion.

KEY TERMS

Alginate	A powder mixed with water to make a smooth paste that is easily set into an elastic material so that a mould can be cast from the patient's mouth
Plaster of paris	A powder mixed with water to form a solid material used to make a model of the patient's mouth

Anatomical articulator	A metal articulator, on which the plaster of Paris models are placed, to mimic the patient's mastication movements
Face bow	Part of the articulator that is used to record the position of the upper occlusion rim in relation to the mandibular condyles (see Chapter 2)
Composition	A solid stick of impression compound that is softened to become a malleable compound, used to build up the peripheral rims of special trays
Edentulous	The absence of any teeth in the mouth
Sheet wax	Sheet of pink wax, used to take bite registration during denture construction
Willis bite gauge	Measuring instrument used to measure the facial height and contour, when constructing a full or partial denture
Wax knife	Blunt knife used to smooth and shape the wax during the wax bite stage of denture construction
Bunsen burner	Used in conjunction with a wax knife, in the dental surgery
Lecron carver	Slim and narrow knife, used often to mark the wax bite centre-line and for fine trimming of dentures at the wax and try-in stages
Acrylic baseplates	Made from shellac or acrylic to construct special trays
Rest seats/ occlusal rests	When a groove is cut into the occlusal surface on adjacent teeth for support during design of partial dentures. Composite restoration material can be used to build a suitable 'seat' up if the occlusal surface is unsuitable; other forms of rest seats are incisal and on the cingulum

Clasps	When a partial denture is designed, and the chrome cobalt sickle-shaped clasps are designed to fit around adjacent teeth to give additional support (can also be used on removable orthodontic appliances)
Chrome cobalt	Combination of chrome and cobalt, used to construct the metal used for dentures and orthodontic appliances
Acrylic	Polymeric material used to construct dentures and orthodontic appliances (Fig. 12.3)
Ulcer	Small area of inflammation that occurs when there has been slight trauma or a reduction in the working of the immune system; can last for up to three weeks
Angular cheilitis	A streptococcal/staphylococcal/candida infection in the folds of the corners of the mouth
Sodium hypochlorite	Solution that can be used to disinfect impressions before being forwarded to the laboratory
Impression trays	Filled with alginate or other impression compounds, these are used during the construction of dentures and orthodontic appliances
Over-denture	Constructed to fit over retained roots and unerupted teeth; invaluable in certain congenital conditions that affect the dentition
Obturator	Fitted to seal a hole in the palate. Commonly used in the treatment of cleft palate, until this can be surgically treated.

13: Endodontics

What is endodontics?

Endodontics, or root canal therapy, is a procedure which involves the removal of the pulp. The pulp chamber is located beneath the enamel and dentine. It contains a whole system of nerves, blood vessels and lymph vessels that help nourish the tooth that pass through the apex of the root canal into the bone. The root canal is widened, cleaned and a root filling is placed that fills the whole length of each root canal in the tooth.

When is endodontic treatment necessary?

Endodontic treatment is carried out as a means to save a tooth once the pulp has become exposed that would otherwise have been extracted. Exposure of the pulp can occur as a result of:

- Trauma - the crown of the tooth is fractured
- Accidental - when the pulp is exposed during cavity preparation
- Carious exposure - decay has passed through the enamel and dentine into the pulp chamber.

Endodontic treatment would also be necessary if a tooth gives a negative response to a vitality test.

Checking whether a tooth is vital

A tooth's vitality should be tested in order to find out which treatment plan will be suitable. If a tooth is alive, a normal restoration or crown would be appropriate. If the tooth is dead, root treatment or extraction would be the correct treatment. Vitality testing can be done in a number of ways:

- Heat (by using gutta percha)
- Cold (by using ice or ethyl chloride)
- Electronic pulp testing
- Pain (drilling a tooth without a local anaesthetic will most certainly identify a vital pulp).

First visit

Equipment and materials required:

- Patients' records
- Rubber dam – to isolate the tooth (see Figs 13.2–8)
- Local anaesthetic
- Radiographs – to determine health of the tooth and later to measure the working length of the root canal.
- High-speed drill and burs – to remove debris and open the canals (access cavity preparation, Fig. 13.1).

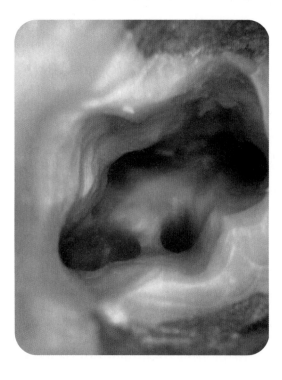

Fig. 13.1 Access cavity – view of the root canal.

- Barbed broach – to remove the nerve within each canal (pulp extirpation).
- Reamers – to clean the canal and remove the dead pulp. Reamers are shaped like a miniature drill bit. Reamers come in a variety of sizes initially to fit and then to enlarge each root canal. They are used in a clockwise direction. They fit on to a slow handpiece, although they can be used manually.

- Files – to enlarge and widen the root canal, to help remove infection and to prepare for the root filling. They have mainly superseded reamers, as they are more flexible. Their blades are cut differently and they are used with more of an 'up-and-down' motion as opposed to the rotary motion of a reamer. Files are made from steel although nickel titanium is more popular now. Both files and reamers can be autoclaved, but, because of their size, debris can be difficult to clean, so regular inspection is important between patients. Rubber stops are used on both reamers and files to indicate the working length of the canals.

- Irrigation syringe – a solution of sodium hypochlorite, saline or local anaesthetic is used to wash or irrigate the root canal.

- Paper points – to dry the canal and absorb any infection, using antibiotic liquid.

- Disinfecting solution – to help control infection in conjunction with oral antibiotics.

- Temporary dressing – to seal the access cavity to prevent further debris going into the canals once they have been dressed with disinfectant. Zinc oxide eugenol can be used as a temporary dressing but when a stronger material needs to be used the dentist may prefer a zinc phosphate dressing.

The procedure

- A local anaesthetic is given to the patient to ensure they feel no discomfort.

- An access cavity is made using the high speed drill and burs.

- When all the canals have been located the pulp is removed using a barbed broach (pulp extirpated).

- The length of the canal is determined using a diagnostics radiograph. This is to enable the correct length of the reamers and files to be used when cleaning and widening each canal to the apex.

- The canal is then reamed and filed.

- The root canal is washed with irrigating solution and dried with paper points.

- A portion of a paper point is then soaked in a disinfecting solution and placed in the root canal.
- A temporary dressing is placed to seal the access cavity.
- The dentist may decide to give the patient a course of antibiotics.

Care must be taken if the patient has had any previous allergies to antibiotics or other contraindications to antibiotics before prescribing. Erythromycin can be used in patients sensitive to penicillin and can also be used in conjunction with metronidazole to cover the different types of bacteria (alcohol must not be consumed when taking the latter as vomiting can occur).

Second visit

At this visit the dentist will assess if the tooth is ready to be root filled.

Equipment and material required

- Radiograph - to determine the health of the tooth and detect and residual infection and determine the working length of the root canal if required
- High speed drill and burs - to remove dressing
- Rubber dam
- Excavators
- Reamers
- Locking tweezers
- Irrigating solution
- Luting cement
- Flat plastic instrument
- Bunsen burner
- Suitable filling material
- Paper points
- Files
- Disinfecting solution
- Gutta percha (GP) points - to spread the filling material within the apex and seal before restoration is placed.

The procedure

- The temporary filling is removed using the high speed drill and the access cavity is opened up.

- The paper point is removed and examined by the dentist to see if it is clean dry or if it is wet and discoloured.

- If the paper point is clean and dry and the patient has no further problems the dentist may then decide to root fill the tooth.

- The dentist will ream and file the canal.

- The canal will then be washed with irrigating solution and dried with paper points.

- A suitably sized GP point is selected and measured to the correct length required.

- The luting cement is mixed and applied to the walls of the root canal and also applied to the GP point. A flat plastic instrument is then heated up and excess GP point material is removed.

- A suitable permanent filling is then placed over the access cavity.

- A radiograph is taken to check the length of the root filling which should fill the whole length of the canal but not extend through the apex of the root canal

Isolating the tooth with a rubber dam

The rubber dam is used to isolate the tooth from the rest of the mouth and surrounding moisture when a dry area is required. It protects the patient's airway and avoids inhalation particularly during endodontic treatment as the instruments used are so small and fiddly to handle. The rubber dam is placed around the tooth in the following way:

- A hole is made in a sheet of rubber dam using a rubber dam punch (figs 13.2, 13.3, 13.4).

- The sheet of rubber dam is then placed over the tooth that is being treated (fig 13.5).

- A frame is placed around the rubber dam sheet to keep it taut (fig 13.6).

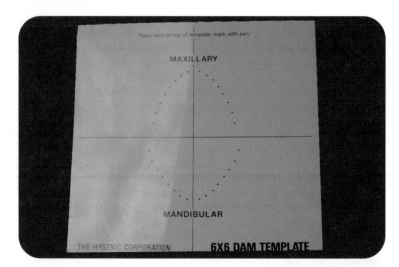

Fig. 13.2 Rubber dam sheet.

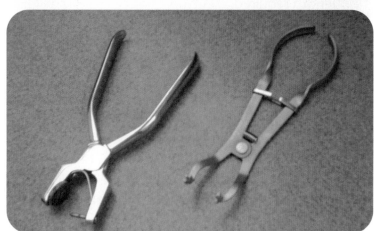

Fig. 13.3 Rubber dam hole punch and forceps.

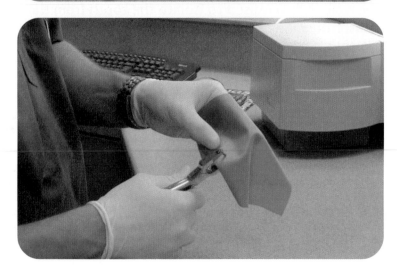

Fig. 13.4 Punching hole in rubber dam.

- Clamps are placed around the tooth to keep the rubber dam sheet in place (fig 13.7).

- Once the rubber dam is in place the tooth is sufficiently isolated prior to treatment (fig 13.8).

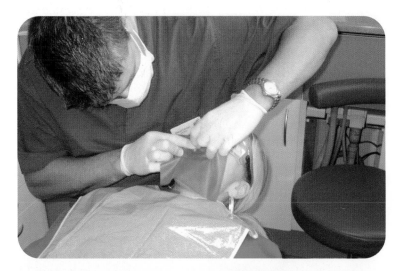

Fig. 13.5 Fitting the rubber dam.

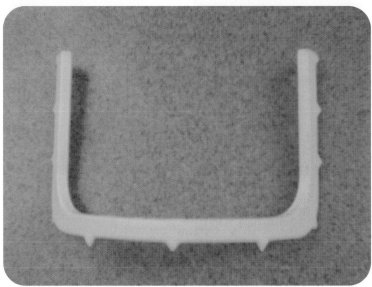

Fig. 13.6 Rubber dam frame.

Fig. 13.7 Variety of rubber dam clamps.

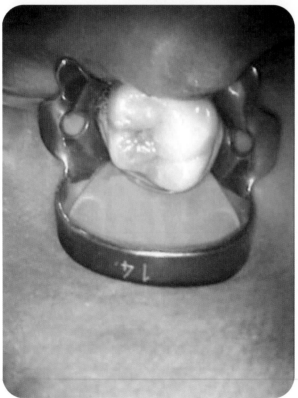

Fig. 13.8 A molar isolated with rubber a dam.

Instruments required for fluoride treatment

- Mirror, probe and tweezers
- Topical fluoride
- Applicator trays or applicator stick
- Aspirator and 3:1 syringe
- Tissues for the patient. The operator may not wish the patient to rinse directly after the treatment as this could reduce the effectiveness of the fluoride treatment.

During the consultation

- Welcome the patient
- Supply the patient with goggles and protective bib
- Support the patient throughout the treatment as this is more often a treatment for younger children
- Aspirate when required by the operator
- Give the patient tissues as required.

Following the treatment

- Clean all the instruments and place in the autoclave
- Wipe down all surfaces with an appropriate cleaning solution such as isopropyl alcohol
- If required by the operator, chart and record the treatment in the patient's records
- Prepare the surgery for the next patient

Apicectomy

An apicectomy is a surgical procedure, performed as a final alternative to the extraction of a non-vital tooth. The procedure is carried out to remove the infected apex and surrounding infected tissue, when:

- because of the shape of the canal, a root filling is not possible (curved roots) or would not be complete

- cement can escape through the apex of the root, causing irritation to the surrounding tissues

- the root canal of a tooth has been blocked during root canal therapy by a broken instrument

- there is an alveolar abscess with a post crown

- there is a cyst

- there is a fracture of the apical one-third of a root.

THE DENTAL NURSE'S ROLE IN PREPARATION FOR THE PROCEDURE

- The patient notes, charts and radiographs should be made ready. As this is a surgical procedure, a sterile operative field is required.

- All required instruments, which have previously been autoclaved, should be placed on either a sterile tray or a towel. Items such as the sterile scalpel blade, swabs and suture pack (local anaesthetic cartridges, needle, handpiece and burs) should be opened and dropped on to the sterile site without touching them.

- A bib and protective glasses, mouthwash and tissues should be prepared for the patient.

- Disposable gloves, mask and protective glasses should be made available for the operator and the dental nurse.

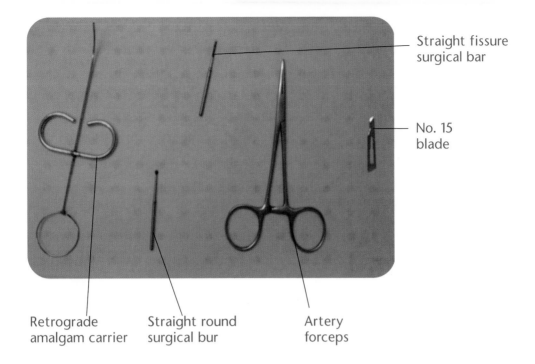

Straight fissure
surgical bar

No. 15
blade

Retrograde
amalgam carrier

Straight round
surgical bur

Artery
forceps

Fig. 13.9 Apicectomy instruments.

Instruments required for the procedure (Fig. 13.9)

- Local anaesthetic syringe, cartridges, needle
- Mirror, probe, tweezers
- Scalpel handle and blade
- Periosteal elevator
- Straight handpiece and burs
- Curettes
- Mitchell's trimmer
- Disposable syringe and sterile saline
- Dissecting forceps
- Needle holder, sutures, scissors
- Fine-bore retrograde amalgam carrier.

Procedure

- Local anaesthetic is administered.

- Using a sterile scalpel blade and handle, a surgical incision is made from the sulcus, around the gingival margin of the tooth, and then back to the sulcus.

- A flap is raised using Mitchell's trimmer and elevator, exposing the underlying bone.

- A window is cut into the bone, using the handpiece and burs to expose the apex of the tooth being treated.

- The apex of the tooth is now removed.

- Using curettes and Mitchell's trimmer all infected tissue is removed.

- The cavity is washed with sterile saline and dried with swabs.

- The end of the root of the tooth is now examined to see if the remaining root filling is deficient. If it is, more root filling is inserted into the canal via the cut end of the root. This could be reinforced zinc oxide eugenol cement, glass ionomer cement or amalgam to seal the end of the root of the tooth.

- The operation site is cleaned of any debris, by syringing with sterile saline.

- The flap is now closed by placing sutures.

- The patient is given postoperative instructions.

- The patient is given an appointment for one week later for a review, when sutures will be removed (if not dissolvable) and a check radiograph taken.

- The patient will be reviewed periodically thereafter.

Pulpotomy

Pulpotomy is performed on children's teeth. The apex on a child's tooth is wider than that on an adult's. Thus when a child has a dental abscess, pressure does not build up as it would in an adult's tooth (as an adult's tooth has a narrow apex, and therefore cannot drain so readily). Pulpotomy means that only the infected part of the pulp is removed and, because the pulp chamber has a very rich blood supply through the open apex, healing can occur effectively.

The procedure is similar to that for root canal treatment in an adult, and so is the cross-infection routine. The infected pulp is removed and calcium hydroxide laid down to encourage new secondary dentine to generate. When this happens, the remaining pulp is covered and protected as it would have been before the infection. Occasionally a full root treatment is required at a later stage.

Pulp capping

Pulp capping is done when a tooth is exposed unexpectedly, and root canal treatment or pulpotomy cannot be done immediately. Calcium hydroxide (or Ledermix) can be placed over the exposure to protect the pulp, and a temporary dressing placed over this until the time when a pulpotomy or root canal treatment can be carried out.

THE DENTAL NURSE'S ROLE IN ROOT CANAL TREATMENT

- Retrieve the patient notes and identify the procedure.

- Prepare the surgery with all the necessary instruments, materials and medicaments.

- Be aware of health and safety at all times, provide personal protective equipment for all staff and patients to help minimise cross-infection, and aspirate when required.

- Be able to anticipate the next stage of any given treatment, so you can prepare and provide adequate and professional continuity in the treatment plan.

- Thoroughly clean and clear away the instruments, medicaments and materials. Wipe surfaces with isopropyl alcohol or similar.

- Sterilise when required in a regularly serviced autoclave – keeping clean and dirty instruments away from each other, as well as from dirty gloves from the previous procedure to prevent contamination of 'clean' gloves.

14

Extractions and Minor Oral Surgery

14: Extractions and Minor Oral Surgery

Extractions may be necessary for the following reasons:

- If there is gross caries present and the tooth is beyond restoration
- Severe periodontal disease (mobility)
- Orthodontic reasons to create space or for adjusting malaligned teeth
- Impacted teeth (eg wisdom teeth or impacted canines)
- Periapical infection from a failed root canal or apicectomy
- Removal of deciduous teeth to encourage the eruption of permanent teeth.

Before any extraction or surgery the patient's medical history must be checked as some medical conditions and medications can affect the treatment. If a patient has a bleeding disorder such as haemophilia, where the blood does not clot, the patient would need to be referred to hospital for treatment. If a patient is on medication such as warfarin that is taken to thin the blood they will bleed for a long period of time. Therefore their general practitioner must be consulted regarding whether the medication can be stopped before extraction to allow for adequate haemostasis or whether they should be referred to hospital.

Before any extraction, the tooth to be extracted is anaesthetised as described in Chapter 8. The lingual or palatal gingivae also need to be anaesthetised.

Extractions can be either simple or complex, ie involving a surgical procedure. In simple extractions a tooth can be removed without the need to remove any bone or soft tissue from around the tooth. The tooth is removed using a combination of elevators and the relevant forceps (see Figs 14.1–14.4 for examples of these). The elevators are used to loosen the tooth in its socket and from the gingival tissue. (This may not be necessary if the tooth is already mobile.) The relevant forceps are used to extract the tooth by pushing up on the tooth with the forceps to disconnect the periodontal membrane. The tooth is then gently manoeuvred from side to side until it comes out.

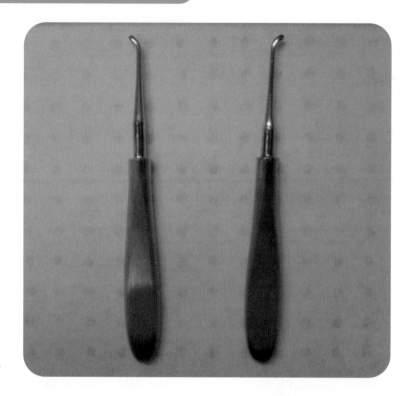

Fig. 14.1
Warwick James'
elevators.

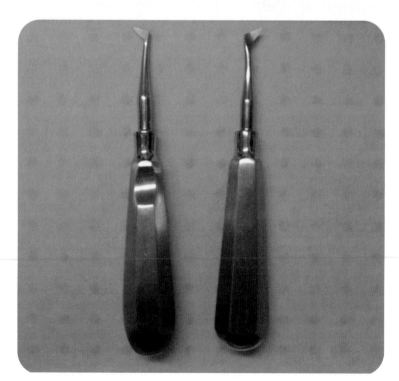

Fig. 14.2 Cryer's
elevators: left
and right.

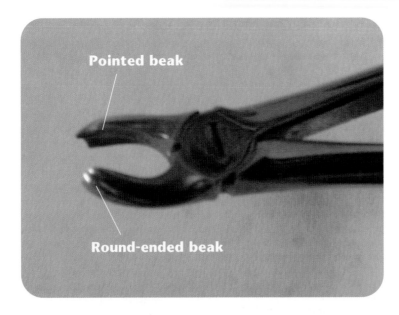

Pointed beak

Round-ended beak

Fig. 14.3 Upper left molar forceps.

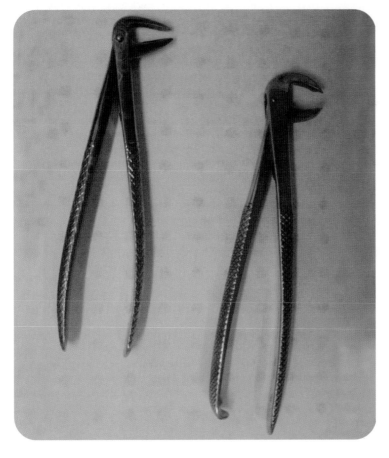

Fig. 14.4 Lower root forceps and lower molar forceps.

Not all extractions are straightforward and sometimes it is necessary to remove a tooth surgically, ie bone and gingivae need to be removed to gain access to the tooth. This is necessary if a tooth had fractured at the root or if it was impacted. The procedure for surgical extraction is described later in the chapter.

Once the tooth has been removed the patient bites on a swab pack to stop any bleeding. They are also given the following postoperative instructions:

- Do not rinse their mouth that day as this will stop a blood clot from forming in the socket.
- Take a painkiller before the anaesthetic wears off and take the stated dose at the recommended time if more is required.
- Avoid hot food and liquids and alcohol.
- Do not smoke for at least 24 hours.
- Avoid any hard, physical activity for the rest of the day.
- If any bleeding occurs fold up a clean cotton handkerchief and bite on it for about 20 minutes to stop the bleeding.
- The following day rinse as often as possible with warm salt water mouthwashes to encourage healing and to keep the area clean.

THE DENTAL NURSE'S ROLE IN EXTRACTIONS

- Ensure that the surgery is prepared for the procedure.
- The patient's record card and radiographs and the instruments required should be ready.
- Make sure that the patient is comfortable throughout the procedure.
- After the procedure give the patient postoperative instructions (see below) and check that they are clean of any blood or debris before they leave the surgery.
- Clean and sterilise all instruments and ensure that used swabs and other clinical waste are disposed of correctly.

Surgical extractions

The instruments required for this procedure are:

- Mouth mirror
- Probe
- Tweezers
- Local anaesthetic cartridge, needle and syringe
- Swann-Morton handle and blades (Fig. 14.5)
- Howarth periosteal elevator
- Osteo Mitchell's trimmer
- Cheek retractor
- Straight handpiece and surgical burs
- Sterile water for irrigation
- Elevators
- Forceps
- Bone rongeurs
- Sutures, either black silk or resorbable
- Ward's needle holders
- Rat-toothed tweezers
- Suture scissors
- Swabs.

Again, it is the nurse's duty to ensure that all instruments and equipment are available for the procedure (Fig 14.6) and that the dentist and the patient are supported throughout.

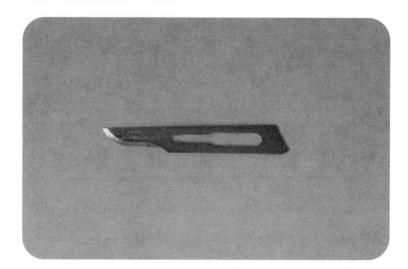

Fig. 14.5 No 15 scalpel blade.

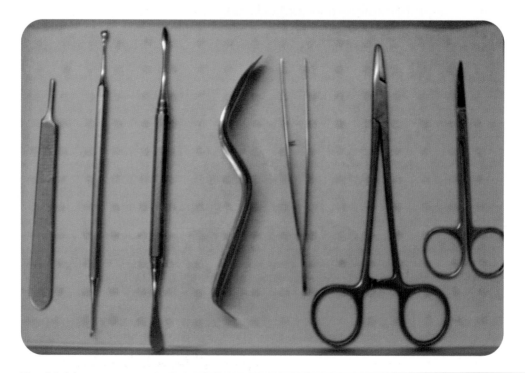

Fig. 14.6 Instrument tray set up for extractions/minor oral surgery. From left to right: Swan Morton handle, osteo Mitchell's trimmer, periosteal elevator, cheek retractor, rat-toothed tweezers/tissue forceps, Ward's needle holders, suture scissors.

The tooth is first anaesthetised and a flap is cut using the blade. This is pushed away from the alveolar bone using the osteo Mitchell's trimmer. The periosteal elevator is used to elevate the gingivae away from the bone. Bone is then removed using the handpiece and surgical burs to allow access to the tooth. Once the tooth has been removed bone rongeurs are used to snip away any loose or jagged pieces of bone, and after this sutures are placed.

THE DENTAL NURSE'S ROLE DURING AND AFTER SURGICAL EXTRACTION

- Irrigate with sterile water during any bone removal to keep it cool

- Aspirate throughout the procedure to remove any water, blood or debris from the patient's mouth and also so that the dentist has a clear field of vision.

- After the procedure, ensure that the patient is given postoperative instructions (see below) and is fit to leave the surgery before they do so.

Besides those mentioned above for simple extractions, postoperative instructions after surgical extraction include:

- After a surgical procedure the patient may experience some discomfort, swelling or bruising.

- The patient should be warned of this before and after the procedure.

- The patient should then be made an appointment for the removal of the sutures unless they are resorbable, in which case they will resorb in about 5–7 days.

Following the procedure, the nurse should clean and sterilise all instruments and disinfect the surgery.

Complications with extractions

Tooth fracture

As stated previously a tooth can fracture during a simple extraction and therefore surgical removal of the tooth would need to be done.

Perforation of the maxillary sinus

This can happen during the extraction of upper molars and premolars where the floor of the sinus lies close to the roots of the teeth. Sometimes the tooth can be pushed into the sinus during extraction and can cause an infection. On extraction of upper molars or premolars with long roots that sit naturally in the sinus, a small opening in the sinus can be created when they are removed. This opening is known as an oroantral fistula. You can tell that a patient has this by asking them to hold their nose and blow down it. If any bubbles appear in the extraction socket then there is an opening between the floor of the sinus and the oral cavity. If it is a small opening it will close naturally; if it is much larger it will need to be surgically closed.

Damage to the inferior dental nerve

This can occur if the roots of the lower molars (especially lower third molars) lie close to or on the nerve canal. If during tooth removal the nerve becomes damaged the patient may experience a numb or tingling sensation around the mandible, lips and tongue. This may be only temporary but can sometimes be permanent. Patients must be warned of this complication before and after the extraction of lower third molars.

Haemorrhage

Primary haemorrhage – This occurs directly after an extraction. Usually bleeding should stop within five minutes of the tooth being removed.

Reactionary haemorrhage – This type of haemorrhage occurs a few hours after the extraction, once the patient has left the surgery. This should be easily controlled by reapplying a swab and some pressure to the socket or suturing if necessary.

Secondary haemorrhage – This occurs where the blood clot is lost from the socket soon after it has formed (usually within 24 hours). The exposed socket then becomes infected and the patient can feel extreme pain. It is commonly known as a dry socket. The socket must be cleaned of any debris and a sedative dressing placed.

Other surgical procedures

Operculectomy

The operculum is the flap of gingiva that covers a third molar tooth while it is erupting. This flap can become tender and sore, so the patient may have difficulty keeping the area clean, and infection can occur. The infection is commonly known as pericoronitis. Thorough cleaning and antibiotics can be used to treat the problem or the flap of skin can be removed. This is known as an operculectomy.

Frenectomy

A frenum is a piece of tissue connecting the gingiva to the lips, cheek or tongue. Frenectomy is the removal of one of these pieces of tissue.

Labial frenectomy – The attachment of the lip to the gingivae between the two front teeth can sometime be too far up, and this can cause a gap to appear between them. This gap is known as a diastema. Removal of the frenum may encourage the gap to close.

Lingual frenectomy – The lingual frenum attaches the tongue to the floor of the mouth. A large frenum may need to be removed as it can limit movement of the tongue and interfere with speech. A frenum can be removed with a scalpel blade followed by suturing or it can be cauterised.

Gingivectomy

Gingivectomy is a surgical treatment done where there has been periodontal disease. In this procedure excess gingiva is cut away, using an instrument known as the Blakes gingivectomy knife. The exposed gingiva is then covered with a zinc oxide eugenol dressing. Once the excess gingiva has been removed with this procedure the teeth can be cleaned thoroughly.

Soft-tissue biopsy

Soft-tissue biopsy involves the removal of a soft-tissue lesion from the lip, cheek or tongue area. Anything that a dentist feels may be at all suspicious should be referred immediately to hospital. If the dentist does the biopsy, the lesion is removed along with a small healthy area surrounding it. The area is then sutured and reviewed after a few days. The cut lesion is put into a biopsy specimen pot and along with a written pathology form sent to the pathology department of the hospital, which will then contact the dentist with the findings.

15 Orthodontics

15: Orthodontics

What is orthodontics?

Orthodontics is the branch of dentistry that is concerned with the growth, development and position of teeth within each jaw. Irregularities in the position, size, and shape of the teeth and lower jaw can be identified by a parent, the patient or the dentist. This condition is known as malocclusion.

Malocclusion

There are several types of malocclusion. Many of them are genetic in their origin. Abnormal jaw size or jaw relationship is the commonest inherited condition, with abnormal size causing increased spacing of teeth. Missing teeth or supernumerary teeth can often be inherited.

Overcrowding

This occurs when the jaws are too small to accommodate the full dentition (32 teeth, 16 in each arch). As space is restricted, teeth will often erupt late and appear to be crooked or to overlap each other (Fig 15.1).

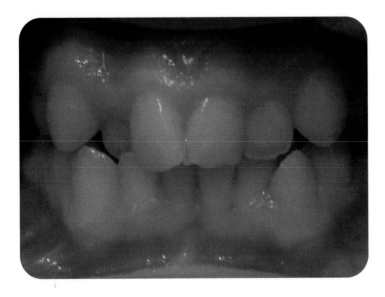

Fig. 15.1 An overcrowded mouth.

Protruding upper incisors

This condition arises from a jaw relationship in which the upper incisors are too far forward in comparison to the lower incisors (Fig 15.2).

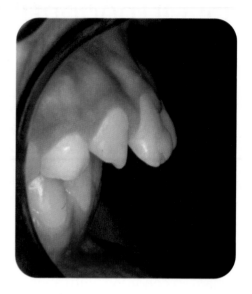

Fig. 15.2 Side view of protruding upper incisors.

Missing teeth

People can be born without the tooth germs present for certain teeth. This condition often affects the upper lateral incisors, second molars, lower central incisors and third molars in both arches. It is known as **hypodontia**. See also Chapter 2.

Soft-tissue habits

Thumb and finger sucking may prevent the permanent teeth from erupting into their correct position in the arch. It can result in the upper anterior teeth protruding forwards (proclination) and the lower anterior teeth lying backwards (retroclination). It can also result in reduced incisal contact of the upper and lower incisors, leading to an open bite (Fig. 15.3).

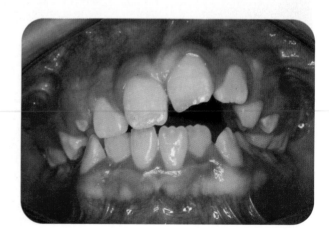

Fig. 15.3 Open bite due to thumb sucking.

Classification of malocclusion (Figs 15.4–15.6)

Angle's classification
Angle's classification is a universally recognised classification system. It is based on how the upper and lower first molars occlude with each other. The mesial buccal groove of the lower first molar should occlude with the mesial buccal cusp of the first upper molar.

Incisor classification

- Class I – the lower incisor edges occlude against the middle third of the palatal surface of the upper incisors.

- Class II division 1 – the lower incisor edges lie close to the cingulum of the upper incisors, the upper incisors are proclined, and there is increased overjet and overbite.

- Class II division 2 – overbite is greater than 50%, so there is an increased overbite. Upper central incisors tilt backwards contacting with lower incisors.

- Class III – when the lower jaw develops further forward than normal. The chin appears to be too far forward, and the lower incisors occlude in front of the upper incisors.

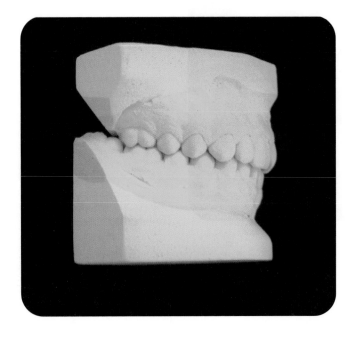

Fig. 15.4 Class I malocclusion.

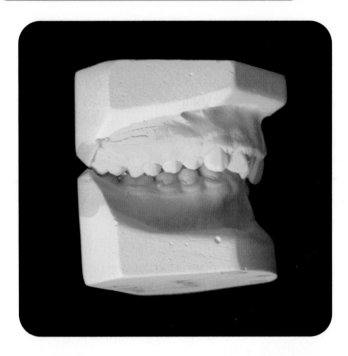

Fig. 15.5 Class II
malocclusion.

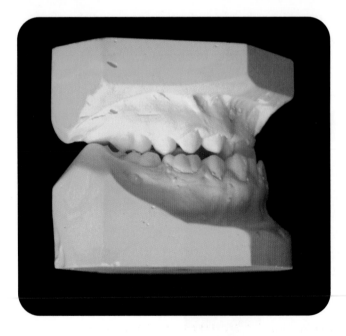

Fig. 15.6 Class III
malocclusion.

How can malocclusion be treated?

Orthodontic treatment is carried out to:

- improve the appearance of teeth

- improve the position of teeth

- improve and restore the function of teeth

- remove stagnation areas, thereby allowing the person to clean each surface of the tooth and the gingivae correctly

- make the patient feel happier about their appearance, thereby in some cases improving their self-esteem.

Extractions

In some cases when either jaw is too small to accommodate a full dentition, crowding and irregular positioning of teeth can occur. Incisors can overlap, canines may become labially displaced, and premolars can be lingually (in lower arch) and palatally (in upper arch) displaced.

To create sufficient space the orthodontist may decide to extract teeth. The commonest teeth to be extracted for this purpose are the first premolars. Even though spaces will be created by extraction, thereby allowing crowded teeth to straighten, appliances will still be necessary to reposition the teeth in satisfactory alignment.

Moving teeth

A light and constant force on a tooth can move it without causing damage to the root of the tooth or the supporting structures. In the alveolar bone, which forms the tooth sockets, such forces induce re-modelling of the bone. Where pressure is applied and is continuous, the alveolar bone lining the socket is resorbed by osteoclasts, allowing the tooth root to move. Odontoblasts then lay down bone, allowing the tooth to be fully supported in its new position.

There are two methods used by the orthodontist to move teeth:

- Tipping – force is applied to the crown of the tooth only (removable appliance)

- Rotation and bodily movement – forces are applied, causing the crown and the root to move (fixed appliance).

Risks of orthodontic treatment

- Root resorption may occur following orthodontic treatment

- Decalcification of enamel around fixed brackets. As patients usually wear orthodontic appliances for long periods of time, ranging from many months to years, their oral hygiene needs to be maintained to a very high standard and their diet needs to be monitored – wherever possible – to eliminate sugars in foods and drinks. Acidic drinks also need to be avoided. Decalcification can occur when oral hygiene has not been maintained and sugar intake has not been controlled while a person is wearing a fixed appliance.

Orthodontic treatment planning

Orthodontic treatment takes place over an extended period of time and usually depends on the patient's malocclusion, age, growth and development. Therefore each patient's treatment is individualised. The orthodontist will assess each patient with regard to:

- their desire for treatment

- parental support (when applicable)

- patient cooperation

- strict oral hygiene and dietary discipline over a long period of time

- commitment to ensuring that all appointments for treatments are kept.

Patients may also have to take an active role in their own treatment, eg activating appliances, and parents in ensuring that appliances are worn and the orthodontist's instructions are rigidly followed. Parents also need to realise and to agree that their child will have to have time off school or college to accommodate their treatment appointments.

Orthodontic consultation and diagnosis

Patients are usually referred by their own general dental practitioner to see an orthodontist to determine the need for orthodontic treatment. At this initial appointment a full orthodontic examination is carried out, including:

- a detailed examination of teeth
- overbite and overjet measurements
- assessment of the effects of lip, tongue and swallowing actions
- evidence of overcrowding in each arch
- evidence of teeth that may be rotated
- evidence of retained deciduous teeth
- evidence of centre-line shifts in either the upper or the lower arch.

Cephalometric radiographs, orthopantomograms (OPG) and occlusal radiographs (see Chapter 7) may be taken before the initial examination to enable the orthodontist to be able to see the position of all erupted teeth and the presence of unerupted teeth in each arch. The radiographs will also show where teeth are missing, and any supernumerary teeth or other abnormalities.

Study models

Alginate impressions of each arch and a wax bite are taken, and from these study models of the patient's teeth are made. The study models are used by orthodontists to examine the malocclusion from all angles, which allows them to decide and formulate the correct treatment plan.

Throughout the patient's orthodontic treatment other study models may be made to allow the orthodontist to record the progress of the patient's treatment.

Photographs

The orthodontist may decide to take a series of photographs, again to use as a record to show the position of the teeth and their appearance at the beginning of treatment, and to record progress at various stages of the patient's treatment, through to its conclusion.

Once a full orthodontic examination has been carried out, the orthodontist will formulate a suitable treatment plan. They will need to explain the treatment plan to the patient and their parent/guardian, and establish whether or not they are prepared to commit themselves fully to the course of the treatment.

Instruments and equipment

- Mirror, probe (for examination of the oral cavity)
- Ruler (to measure the overjet and overbite)
- Dividers (to measure the width of teeth or to measure spaces between teeth or diastema)
- Alginate impression material (and measures)
- Mixing bowl, spatula
- Fixative
- Range of upper and lower disposable impression trays and handles
- Wax (for bite registration)
- Laboratory request form
- A sealable plastic bag
- Safety glasses and bib for the patient
- Disposable gloves, masks and protective glasses for the dental nurse and the orthodontist
- Mouthwash and tissues for the patient
- Hand mirror for the patient.

THE DENTAL NURSE'S ROLE IN ORTHODONTIC CONSULTATIONS

Before the consultation

- Ensure that all work surfaces are suitably disinfected.
- Ensure that all equipment and instruments listed above, and previously sterilised, are available for use.
- Set out patient notes, including referral letter, radiographs, completed medical questionnaire, details of medical and dental history, and charting.
- Prepare a suitable range or both intraoral and extraoral X-ray films and ensure that both the X-ray machine and the processing equipment are fully working and ready for use. Also prepare X-ray film holders and X-ray envelopes to store the radiographs in, once the films have been taken and processed.

- If photographs are taken, as they routinely are at this stage, the nurse will also need to ensure that the camera is available and prepared.

During the consultation

- Greet the patient.

- Supply them with a bib and protective glasses.

- Provide and pass appropriate instruments to the dentist.

- Record information onto patient notes, as dictated to you by the orthodontist, accurately and completely.

- Prepare and mix the alginate impression material correctly and load the impression trays.

- Prepare the wax for the wax bite.

- Correctly handle and disinfect the impressions and wax bite once they have been removed from the patient's mouth.

- Ensure that the impressions and wax bite are secured in the laboratory bag and all instructions and patient details have been entered on the laboratory request form.

- Help the patient with mouth washing.

- Prepare and hand suitable radiographs to the orthodontist. Correctly process the radiographs taken.

- Assist the orthodontist while photographs are taken.

- At the end of the appointment help the patient clean up and remove the bib and protective glasses. Ensure that they have their next appointment.

After the consultation

- Dispose of all waste, safely and correctly.

- Prepare all instruments for sterilisation, then carry out the sterilisation process.

- Ensure that all work surfaces are disinfected.

- Ensure that the laboratory work is put out ready for collection by the dental laboratory.

- Prepare the surgery for the next patient.

Removable appliances

Removable appliances are used in orthodontic treatment to:

- tip teeth
- reduce overbites
- act as passive space retainers following extractions
- act as retainers after fixed appliances have been removed.

Removable appliances are constructed with an acrylic plate (Fig. 15.7). Active components may consist of:

- a stainless steel wire (to move and reposition the teeth in the arch; Fig. 15.8)
- finger springs (to retract premolars and canines)
- T springs and Z springs (to procline teeth)
- buccal canine retractors (to pull canines back into the correct position in the upper arch after extraction of premolars has created the required space)
- a midline screw (to correct cross-bites — the patient will have to follow the dentist's instructions and activate the screw twice a week, with the use of a key).

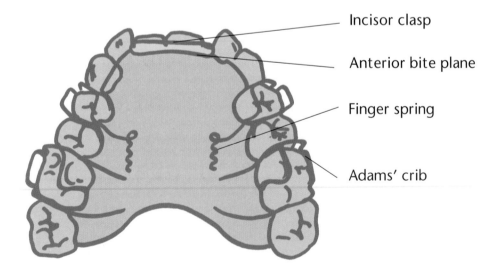

Incisor clasp

Anterior bite plane

Finger spring

Adams' crib

Fig. 15.7 An upper removable appliance.

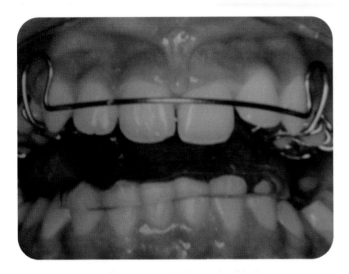

Fig. 15.8 An upper removable appliance in the mouth.

First appointment

First the patient has an appointment with the orthodontist during which impressions are taken. From these impressions the removable appliance is constructed in the dental laboratory. Then, at the second appointment, the orthodontist will fit the removable appliance and instruct the patient on wearing the appliance, care of the appliance, and oral health and diet. The orthodontist will also make sure that the patient is able to take the appliance out and then put it back in again correctly.

THE DENTAL NURSE'S ROLE IN ORTHODONTIC TREATMENT WITH REMOVABLE APPLIANCES – FIRST APPOINTMENT

Before the procedure

- Ensure that all work surfaces have been disinfected and all instruments have been sterilised.

- Keep ready the patient notes, radiographs, study models and photographs.

- Prepare a suitable range of instruments, equipment and materials (see below).

During the procedure

- Assist the dentist and support the patient.
- Pass instruments to the dentist as required.
- Correctly measure out and mix the alginate impression material and load the trays as required.
- Support the patient while the impressions are in the mouth.
- Correctly handle the impressions after they have been removed from the patient's mouth, disinfecting them correctly.
- Help the patient with mouthwash and remove any impression material from the face.
- Complete laboratory instructions on to the laboratory instruction card as dictated by the dentist.
- Ensure that the patient is given an appointment to have the removable appliance fitted.

After the procedure

- Safely dispose of clinical waste correctly.
- After treatment remove all instruments and prepare them correctly for sterilisation.
- Ensure that laboratory work is ready for collection by the dental laboratory.
- Ensure that the patient notes have been fully written up, showing today's treatment.

Instruments required for first appointment

- Mirror and probe
- Alginate impression material
- Range of impression trays
- Fixative
- Mixing bowl and spatula
- Laboratory instruction card
- Sealable laboratory bags.

Second appointment – fitting the removable appliance

At this appointment, the orthodontist will fit the patient with their new removable appliance. The orthodontist will check the removable appliance to ensure that the instructions have been fully carried out and the appliance is intact. They will then insert the appliance to make sure that it fits the patient correctly.

Any adjustments to the appliance are now made. After marking any areas that need adjustment with a marking pencil, the acrylic is trimmed with an acrylic bur in a slow handpiece. The incisor clasp and Adams' cribs can be adjusted with Adams' universal pliers. Adams' spring-forming pliers are used to adjust the finger springs and T and Z springs.

Once the appliance fits comfortably and correctly the orthodontist will explain and demonstrate to the patient how to take it out and put it in correctly. Instructions given to the patient at the first appointment are now reinforced: how to care for their new appliance, the importance oral hygiene, which foods and drinks to be avoided, and the importance of keeping all future appointments for adjustments to the appliance.

Instructions to patient on fitting a removable appliance

- Make sure that the appliance is worn as directed by the orthodontist.

- Remove the appliance and clean it after each meal, using a toothbrush and toothpaste.

- Brush teeth after every meal, before inserting the appliance again – use a flouride mouthwash.

- Try to avoid all sugary, sticky foods and sugary drinks.

- Attend all appointments for adjustment of the appliance.

- It is important that general dental health be maintained, with the usual check-ups and treatment with the general dental practitioner.

- If the appliance is removed, at meal times or during PE lessons at school, ensure that the appliance is stored in a suitable rigid container to avoid damage.

- There may be some discomfort initially when wearing the appliance. The appliance may feel tight and the patient may experience some problems with speaking. These problems will pass quite quickly.

- If problems do continue or if the appliance breaks contact the orthodontist's practice straight away.

It is important to ensure that the patient and the parent fully understand all instructions that are given, as failure to follow them fully could lead to failure of the treatment.

THE DENTAL NURSE'S ROLE IN ORTHODONTIC TREATMENT WITH REMOVABLE APPLIANCES – SECOND APPOINTMENT

Before the procedure

- Ensure that the surgery work surfaces have been fully disinfected and equipment has been suitably sterilised.

- Lay out the patient notes, radiographs, study models and photographs.

- Put out ready the completed laboratory work – the removable appliance – ensuring that the appliance has been disinfected before the patient tries it on.

During the procedure

- Assist the dentist and support the patient through this procedure.

- Greet the patient and ensure that they are wearing a bib and the protective glasses.

- Monitor the patient throughout the procedure.

- Pass instruments and equipment to the orthodontist as required.

- Assist and support the patient with inserting and removing the new appliance.

- Assist with oral hygiene instructions as requested by the orthodontist.

- Give advice on using the expansion screw (if applicable).

- Give the patient post-insertion instructions – verbal and written instructions, as requested by the orthodontist.

- Ensure that the patient notes have been fully completed as requested by the orthodontist.

- Ensure that the patient has been given a further appointment to attend for adjusting the appliance.

After the procedure

- Ensure that all clinical waste is correctly handled and disposed of.

- Ensure that all instruments are prepared for sterilisation and that the process is correctly carried out.

- Ensure that all work surfaces are suitably disinfected.

- Ensure that the surgery is prepared for the next patient.

Instruments for fitting a removable appliance (Fig. 15.9)

- Mirror

- Probe

- Tweezers

- Ruler and dividers

- Adams' universal pliers (for adjusting Adams' cribs)

- Spring-forming pliers (for adjusting springs)

- Heavy wire cutters (Mauns, for cutting wires if necessary)

- Acrylic trimming burs and straight handpiece (for trimming the acrylic baseplate)

- Chinagraph pencil (to make any areas of adjustment on the appliance)

- Hand mirror for the patient

- Instruction sheet for the patient on how to 'care for the appliance'

- Bib/protective glasses/mouthwash/tissues (for the patient)

- Disposable masks/gloves/protective glasses (for the dental nurse and orthodontist)

- Rigid container (for the removable appliance to be stored in safely).

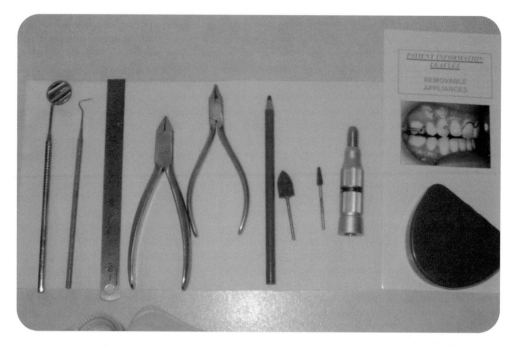

Fig. 15.9 Instruments used for fitting a removable appliance.

Patients who have been fitted with removable appliances will need to visit the orthodontist regularly to have the appliance adjusted and the condition reviewed.

Functional appliances

Functional appliances (Fig 15.10) are also removable appliances, but differ in their action. There are several different types of functional appliance.

The twin-block appliance

This is the commonest functional appliance. It is made of separate upper and lower acrylic plates that are held in place in the patient's mouth by Adams' cribs. Each plate is constructed with posterior acrylic blocks. The appliance when worn encourages the patient to push their mandible forward. Thus this appliance is used to treat moderate-to-severe class II division 1 malocclusions (see above). The upper and lower plates occlude together properly and comfortably only when the jaw is positioned in a forward position. Unlike other functional appliances, the twin block is intended to do this, and must be worn at all times (including meal times).

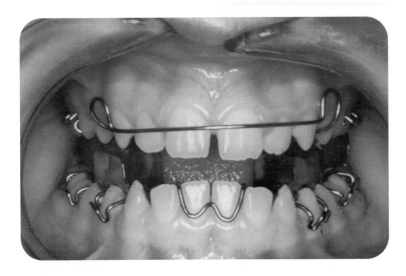

Fig. 15.10
Functional
appliance.

The Andresen appliance

This is constructed of one block of acrylic that fits both the mandible and the maxilla. This type of functional appliance is also used for patients with a class II division 1 malocclusion. The appliance opens the patient's bite and positions the mandible in a forward position. Patients are instructed to wear this appliance as much as possible during the day and all night, every night. Patients are allowed to remove the appliance for eating or when taking part in sporting activities.

The Frankel appliance

This is also most commonly used in patients with class II division 1 malocclusions. The appliance is constructed of acrylic pads that hold the cheeks and lips away from the teeth. Stainless steel wires hold the acrylic pads together. The patient is allowed to take the appliance out at meal times and when taking part in sporting activities.

Treatment procedures

Treatment procedures for each type of functional appliance described above follow the same schedule of appointments as the other removable appliances:

- Impressions and construction of the appliance
- Fitting of the appliance
- Adjustment of the appliance.

THE DENTAL NURSE'S ROLE

The nurse's duties are the same as the duties listed for removable appliances.

As with all removable appliances, their success depends very much on the level of commitment by the patient. If the patient persistently does not follow the instructions of the orthodontist, and does not wear the appliance, or continues to miss adjustment appointments, treatment may be ultimately discontinued before it has been completed. Usually all orthodontic patients are warned by the orthodontist at the beginning of their treatment that failure to comply with the orthodontist's instructions will result in their treatment being terminated.

Fixed appliances

Fixed appliances (Figs 15.11 and 15.12), unlike removable appliances, are assembled in the patient's mouth while they are in the dental chair:

- Brackets are bonded directly to the labial or buccal surface of the patient's teeth, using either glass ionomer cement or composite after acid etching.

- Bands, which may be used on molar teeth, are cemented in place with glass ionomer cement or a light cure cement.

- Archwires, usually pre-formed and made from stainless steel or flexible nickel-titanium, are secured to the slots in the brackets and threaded through the tubes on the bands, and are held in position with the use of wire ligatures or elastic modules.

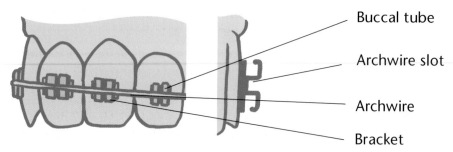

Buccal tube

Archwire slot

Archwire

Bracket

Fig. 15.11 Parts of fixed appliance.

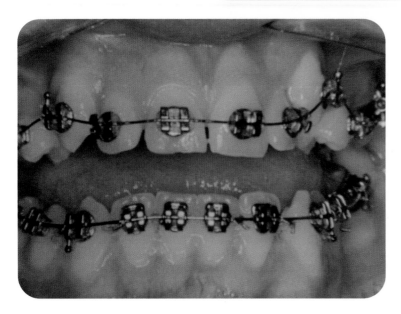

Fig. 15.12 Fixed appliance in the mouth.

Fixed appliances move the root of the tooth through bone, enabling whole teeth to be moved. Greater forces can thereby be applied, including those necessary to derotate teeth.

Stages of treatment

Before a fixed appliance is inserted, the patient will have been for an initial consultation appointment. Once it is decided that the patient requires a fixed appliance, the treatment plan will be explained to the patient and parent.

The orthodontist will explain what this form of treatment involves, roughly how long the patient will need to wear the fixed appliance for, how often the patient will need to attend to have the appliance adjusted, and what will happen after the fixed appliance has been removed. The patient will need to wear a retainer after treatment has been completed to ensure that the teeth do not drift.

Separators

If a patient is having bands cemented on the first molars as part of the fixed appliance, they may need to have separators (elastics) placed between the molars to create enough space for the band to be placed.

THE DENTAL NURSE'S ROLE IN PREPARING THE SURGERY FOR SEPARATORS

- Ensure that cross-infection control is maintained (as described for previous treatments).
- Put out the patient notes, study models, radiographs and photographs.
- Prepare the instruments and materials for treatment (see below).
- Assist the dentist and support the patient through this procedure.
- Monitor the patient throughout the treatment.
- Pass instruments and materials, as instructed by the dentist.
- Aspirate the treatment area as required.
- Reassure and support the patient, while the separating elastics are placed.
- Give post-insertion instructions to the patient, as instructed by the dentist.
- Ensure that the patient is given written instructions.
- Ensure that the patient has their next appointment booked to have the fixed appliance fitted.

After the patient has left the surgery the dental nurse should:

- Dispose of clinical waste correctly.
- Prepare instruments for sterilisation and carry out the sterilisation procedure.

Instruments and equipment

- Mirror/probe/tweezers
- Ruler and divider
- Separating elastics – which will be placed between the molars to push the teeth apart enough to create space for the band to be placed

- Separating pliers
- 3-in-1 tip (water and air)
- Bib/safety glasses/mouthwash for the patient
- Protective glasses/disposable gloves/masks for the dental nurse and orthodontist
- Hand mirror and instruction sheet
- In assisting the dentist and supporting the patient, the dental nurse will be required to follow the points in the box.

THE DENTAL NURSE'S ROLE DURING ASSEMBLING AND FITTING OF THE FIXED APPLIANCE

Preparation of the surgery

This will follow the same procedure as already described, and the dental nurse will need to keep ready the patient notes, radiographs, study materials and photographs. The dental nurse will be required to prepare the equipment and materials for the procedure as listed below.

During the procedure

- Assist the dentist and support the patient through this procedure.
- Ensure that the patient is wearing the bib and protective glasses.
- Monitor the patient throughout the treatment.
- Pass instruments and equipment as required by the dentist.
- Prepare and mix materials/cements.
- Place cement on to the correct surfaces of the brackets and bands.
- Aspirate the treatment area.
- Control moisture throughout the treatment.
- Maintain patient comfort throughout the procedure.

- Give post-insertion instructions to the patient as requested by the dentist.
- Give support to the patient following the procedure.
- Ensure that the patient has another appointment for adjustment of the appliance.

After the procedure

This will follow the same procedure as already described.

Instruments used in fitting fixed appliances (Fig. 15.13)

- Mirror and probe
- Selection of suitable archwires (pre-formed)
- Selection of brackets and bands (for cementing on to the teeth)
- Howe pliers (for holding the archwire)
- Bracket-holding pliers (for holding each bracket)
- Distal end cutters (for cutting the archwire)
- Band-seating instruments (these can include a bite stick and band pusher)
- Band-removing pliers (in case the band needs to be repositioned)
- Light wire pliers (for bending the archwire)
- Ligature tucker and cutters
- Handpiece and polishing rubber cup
- Prophylaxis paste
- Acid etch/bonding solution and composite
- Curing light and shield
- Glass ionomer cement
- Aspirator tip
- 3-in-1 tip (air and water)
- Cheek retractors

- Saliva ejector
- Cotton-wool balls
- Bib/protective glasses/mouthwash (for patient)
- Disposable gloves/mask/protective glasses (for dental nurse and dentist)
- Hand mirror
- Comfort wax (for patient to put on any area of the appliance that is causing discomfort).

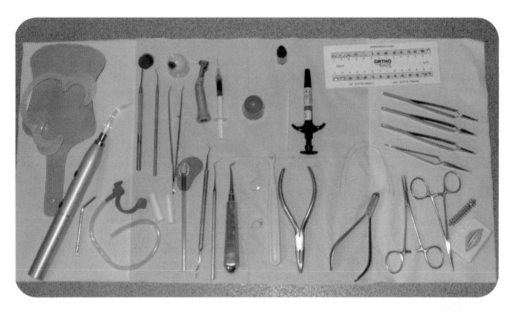

Fig. 15.13 Instruments used in fitting fixed appliance.

Post-insertion instructions for a patient with a fixed appliance

Post-insertion instructions should be detailed, as failure to comply with them will have a detrimental effect on the treatment. Where young adults are involved it is also essential that instructions are explained to the parent. Most orthodontic practitioners have printed instruction leaflets that will be given to patients to enable them to remember all the instructions explained to them. It is also very important to allow the patient and parent suitable opportunities to ask any questions or discuss any part of the instructions that they do not understand. The post-insertion instructions should include:

- Toothbrushing instructions – the correct type of brush and paste to be used and the correct method of brushing the teeth and the appliance should be demonstrated. The use of interdental aids and flouride mouthwash should be discussed. The frequency and timing of toothbrushing should also be explained.

- Dietary advice – it is essential that the patient should be aware of what foods and drinks should be avoided, and why this is necessary. Patients should also be aware of the fact that biting into apples, crusty bread, etc, may actually knock brackets off the teeth, so it will be necessary to explain that some foods need to be cut up into small pieces before they are eaten. Diet analysis may also be carried out to highlight to the patient how their eating habits need to change.

- Care of the appliance – it is essential that the patient and the parent are fully aware of the importance of adequate care for their appliance, as failure to do so will either delay the treatment or result in the treatment failing completely. Patients should be instructed that if any part of the appliance becomes loose or comes off they need to return to the surgery straight away.

- Maintenance of their normal dental check-ups and treatment – patients need to be aware of the importance of attending their own dentist regularly.

- Most patients who have a fixed appliance fitted will experience some pain or discomfort initially. Patients need to understand that this is normal and will eventually subside. The orthodontist usually supplies the patient with wax that can be applied to any area of the appliance that is causing problems. The patient needs to be shown how to use the wax.

Patients and their parents need to understand the importance of attending all future adjustment appointments. Appointments should be written on an appointment card and given to the patient.

Adjustment of fixed appliances

Patients undergoing fixed appliance orthodontic treatment usually visit the orthodontist approximately every 6–8 weeks to have the appliance adjusted. This can involve further brackets or bands being inserted. Arch-wires are changed and become progressively thicker and stronger. Wire ligatures and elastic modules are also replaced.

At each adjustment appointment the orthodontist will also review the patient's condition and record how much the teeth have moved.

Headgear

In some cases of orthodontic treatment extraoral traction to the appliance may be required from headgear (Fig. 15.14) worn by the patient. In this way additional force is exerted on to the appliance from outside the patient's mouth. Patients usually wear the headgear in the evenings and while they sleep. The external headgear is attached to the appliance by a face bow, which is held in place by inserting the ends into buccal tubes or hooks on the appliance inside the mouth.

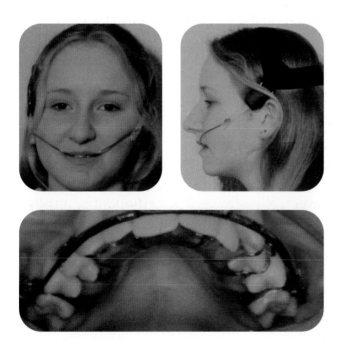

Fig. 15.14 Headgear in place.

Removal of a fixed appliance

Once the planned orthodontic treatment has been completed the fixed appliance has to be removed. An appointment will be arranged for the patient to have the appliance removed and final study models, radiographs, and photographs will be taken. The patient will also be supplied with a retainer, which can be:

- A fixed retainer, which is bonded to the lingual or palatal surfaces of the teeth. It is usually left in place indefinitely after the fixed appliance has been removed.

- A removable retainer: this is a removable orthodontic appliance that is worn by the patient under the orthodontist's instructions, usually full-time at first then just at night, until the orthodontist says that it does not have to be worn anymore.

THE DENTAL NURSE'S ROLE DURING REMOVAL OF A FIXED APPLIANCE

Preparation of the surgery

- Ensure that all surfaces should have been disinfected.

- Ensure that the instruments required have been previously autoclaved.

- Ensure that all materials and equipment are ready.

- Put out the patient notes, radiographs, study models and photographs.

- Ensure that the instruments, equipment and materials for the procedure (listed below) are ready, and handle each item correctly and safely to avoid personal injury or damage.

During the procedure

- Assist the orthodontist and support the patient during the treatment.

- Ensure that the patient is wearing the protective glasses and bib.

- Reassure and support the patient throughout the treatment.

- Suitably answer any questions that the patient may ask.

- At all times monitor the patient throughout the appointment.

- Supply the orthodontist with instruments and equipment when instructed to do so.

- Maintain a clear field of vision and control moisture throughout the procedure.

- Assist the orthodontist with etching and bonding.

- Assist suitably with supplying and applying composite material.

- Activate and operate the curing light when required to do so.

- Prepare impression trays.

- Suitably measure out and mix impression material.

- Correctly handle impressions after they have been taken.

- Complete laboratory instructions as directed by the orthodontist.

- Assist the orthodontist and support the patient while radiographs are being taken.

- Ensure that films are correctly developed.

- Ensure that patient details are entered on to the X-ray envelope correctly and that films are suitably stored.

- Ensure that patient notes have been fully written up, as instructed by the orthodontist.

- Make sure that any post-procedure instructions are fully explained to the patient.

- Ensure that the patient is aware of when they have to attend for a review appointment.

After the procedure

- Ensure that all waste is disposed of correctly.

- Prepare all instruments and equipment for sterilisation and ensure that all work surfaces are disinfected

- Make sure that the patient's laboratory work is ready to be picked up by the dental laboratory

- Prepare the surgery for the next patient.

Instruments and equipment

For removing the fixed appliance (Fig. 15.15)

- Mirror/probe/tweezers (for removing the appliance)
- Debanding pliers (for removing brackets and bands)
- Howe's pliers (for securing the archwire)
- Distal end cutters (for cutting the wire)
- Mitchell's trimmer (for removing cement from teeth)
- Burs (for removing composite from teeth)
- Polishing cup and paste (cleaning teeth)
- Aspirator tip (to control moisture and maintain a clear field of vision)
- 3-in-1 tip (for washing and drying the operation site)
- Contra-angle handpiece
- Cotton-wool balls (for insertion of retainer)
- Acid-etch/composite/bonding solution (to hold the retaining wire in position)
- Curing light and shield
- Selection of thin wire or twist wire (for lingual or palatal surface of anterior teeth, which when cemented in place acts as a retainer, preventing the teeth from drifting out of line).

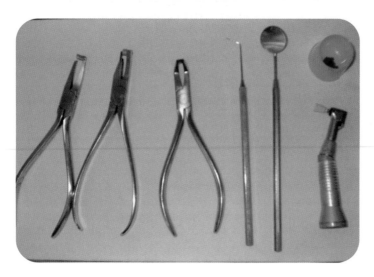

Fig. 15.15
Instruments used in removing a fixed appliance.

For insertion of a removable appliance that acts as a retainer:

- Removable appliance (retainer)
- Adams' universal pliers and spring-forming pliers (for adjusting the cribs)
- Chinagraph pencil (to mark areas of the acrylic that require adjustment)
- Handpiece and acrylic burs (for adjusting the acrylic)
- Hand mirror
- Instruction sheet for patient
- Container for appliance safety.

For final records at the end of their treatment:

- Range of disposable impression trays
- Fixative
- Alginate impression material
- Suitable powder and water measures
- Mixing bowl and spatula
- Laboratory instruction form
- Laboratory bag
- Disinfectant (to disinfect impression before sending to the dental laboratory)
- Radiographs (OPG, occlusal, lateral oblique) and envelope
- Camera with film
- Mouthwash and tissues
- Bib and protective glasses for patient
- Disposable mask, gloves and protective glasses for the orthodontist and dental nurse.

KEY TERMS

Angle's classification	Classification of malocclusion based on the relationship of the teeth, mainly how the upper and lower first permanent molars occlude with each other
Anodontia/ hypodontia	Developmental absence of teeth
Articulation	Relationship of the upper and lower teeth within their normal range of movement
Cross-bite	Upper posterior teeth bite together inside the lower teeth, rather than outside them, as they should normally do
Diastema	A natural space between erupted teeth, most commonly occurring between the upper central incisors
Displacement	Malposition of a tooth
Eruption	The natural movement and development of teeth through the bone and mucosa into the oral cavity
Incisor classification	Malocclusion classification which is mainly concerned with the relationship between the upper and lower incisors
Malocclusion	Irregularities in jaw position and/or size, eg overcrowding of teeth due to insufficient room in the mouth for teeth to erupt into their correct position in the arch
Occlusion	Contact between the occlusal surfaces of the teeth in the opposing arches
Overbite	How far the upper incisors vertically overlap the lower incisors
Supernumerary tooth	An extra tooth

16 Dental Implants

16: Dental Implants

A dental implant is a complete replacement for a natural tooth, composed of a small titanium screw placed into the jaw bone, which will support a crown, bridge or denture to replace one or more missing teeth (Figs 16.1 and 16.2).

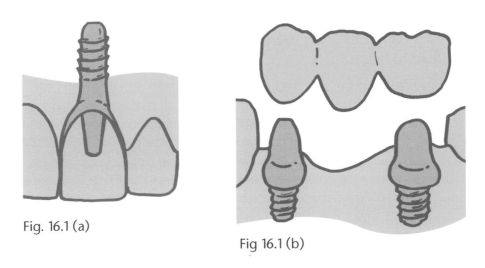

Fig. 16.1 (a)

Fig 16.1 (b)

Fig. 16.1 (a) Single tooth implant and (b) a bridge retained by implants.

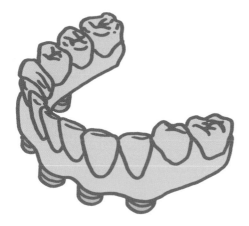

Fig. 16.2 Implant-retained denture.

The advantages of dental implants are:

- When the implant has replaced one tooth there is no effect on the neighbouring teeth.

- Implants can also be used to support a bridge, so eliminating the need for a partial denture.

- Implants can be used to provide support for a full or partial denture to make the denture more secure and comfortable.

Most people can have implants provided that they have good oral health and do not have any general medical complications that prevent them from having surgery.

A patient needs to be assessed to check whether implants will be suitable for them. The assessment includes a full medical and dental history taken, and a full mouth examination including periodontal condition, radiographs and study models. An orthopantomogram (OPG) can be taken to check the levels of bone and the position of certain anatomical features such as the maxillary sinus and the inferior dental nerve. The position of these structures, depending on the bone levels, can sometimes make the placing of implants more complex, thereby increasing the total length of the procedure from start to finish. The bone levels can be reduced if the person has had a tooth extracted or has had periodontal disease.

Bone grafting

A bone graft may be needed because bone levels are sometimes not suitable to house implants after periodontal disease or extraction. Bone can be taken from another part of the body or artificial bone can be used and this will integrate with the natural bone. Once this has integrated the implant can be placed.

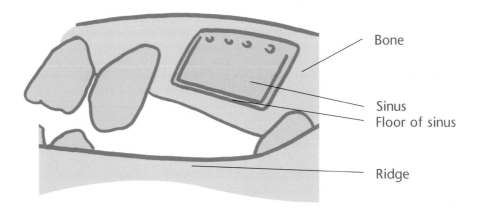

Bone

Sinus
Floor of sinus

Ridge

Fig. 16.4 Sinus lift.

Sinus lift (Fig. 16.4)

This is also known as sinus augmentation. This may be required after upper premolars or molars have been extracted. After extraction the sinus cavity can drift towards the ridge of the upper jaw. If this happens there may not be enough bone in which to place the implants. The membrane of the sinus can be elevated and bone graft material placed where the sinus was. This will then integrate with the natural bone and allow for implants to be placed at a later date.

Inferior dental nerve

It is important to know the position of the inferior dental nerve before implant placement in the lower jaw. If an implant is placed too close to the nerve canal it can become damaged, and the patient can experience permanent numbness in the lower jaw in extreme cases.

When implants are placed this involves a full surgical procedure similar to that described in Chapter 14 and implant equipment would be used.

THE DENTAL NURSE'S ROLE IN IMPLANT SURGERY

Before the procedure

- Ensure that the surgery is prepared with all the equipment and materials needed for the procedure.

During the procedure

- Pass the necessary equipment and materials to the dentist when required and aspirate throughout to remove water and debris, so that the dentist has a clear field of vision throughout the procedure and the patient is comfortable.

- You may also be required to retract the cheek or lip when necessary.

- The patient must be monitored during and after the procedure and must not be allowed to leave the surgery until they are fit to do so.

After the procedure

- Ensure that all equipment is cleaned and sterilised and the surgery disinfected.

After the surgery

Once the implant has been placed it will take anything from a few weeks to a few months for the implant to integrate with the jaw bone – usually longer in the lower jaw as the bone is much denser. There are many methods of implant placement and the method used will depend on the type of patient and the dentist's preferences.

Several visits are needed over the next few months to check the healing process and to begin construction of the prosthesis that will be attached to the top of the implant. Once the procedure is complete it is important that meticulous oral hygiene be maintained and that the patient attend for regular examinations and hygiene appointments to ensure that the implant stays healthy.

17/ Managing Patient Appointments and Payments

17: Managing Patient Appointments and Payments

Many dental nurses undertake reception duties either as part of their duties or on a relief basis during a specific time of the day. It is essential that the dental nurse, when fulfilling her reception duties, has:

- A thorough knowledge of the organisation, its structure, and the names, jobs and roles of all the members of staff who work there

- The ability to project a positive image to all patients and visitors to the practice, and to be willing to assist them with their needs

- An excellent understanding of the practice's procedures, especially how to deal with patients and visitors.

The dental practice structure and responsibilities

All patients and visitors report at reception for a reason – they may be making an appointment for treatment for themselves, or on behalf of a family member. They could also be making enquiries about the services that the practice offers or be making a payment for treatment received. It is the dental nurse's responsibility to ensure that each patient's needs are dealt with promptly and efficiently. For doing this, the dental nurse will need to have:

- General information about the practice, such as details of services provided, prices of various treatments that can be carried out

- A good knowledge of the dental procedures offered by the practice

- A list of the staff and their telephone extension numbers

- Information about which dental practitioners are available and the sessions that they operate

- Knowledge regarding the practice's policies for dealing with casual callers or patients who receive emergency treatment

- Knowledge of how to respond in an emergency.

In addition they will need to:

- Know which patients are expected to attend each day and whom they will see

- Be able to read and understand the appointment system, at a glance

- Be able to input or delete patient details when required to do so.

Dealing with hostile visitors

A key skill of reception staff is the ability to cope and deal with patients or visitors who, for whatever reason, may be seen as being hostile. This may be due to the fact that they are angry or annoyed about something that has happened or the way that they have been spoken to or treated.

You should always try to stay calm and find out what the patient is angry or annoyed about. Suggest that the problem be discussed away from the main public area, and at all times bear in mind your own safety. Find out what the patient wants and listen to them. Take notes of the situation if necessary. Look sympathetic and interested in what is being said. Never interrupt the patient with negative statements, such as 'You must be mistaken'. Try not to say or do anything to make the situation worse. Check with a more senior member of staff before making any promises to the patient, and make sure that whatever is agreed with the patient is done quickly.

Ensure that details of the problem are fully recorded in the patient notes. If at any point you feel that the situation is getting out of hand, or that you cannot resolve the problem, ask someone more experienced for help and advice.

Projecting a positive image

It is very important that the dental nurse maintains a positive image while working both in the surgery and at reception. Appropriate clothes, careful grooming and a high level of personal hygiene are, of course, extremely important. However, being friendly and welcoming to all patients and visitors is of equal importance. All patients and visitors should be greeted with a smile and a welcome, and at all times be treated with courtesy. Patients should feel that you have time for them.

In this unit of the NVQ, you will need to show competence in managing appointment systems within the practice. It is important therefore that in fulfilling reception duties the dental nurse should be fully aware of the practice procedures when making appointments for patients, or on behalf of patients. Throughout the course of the working day, appointments for treatments will be requested by:

- The patient or a relative acting on a patient's behalf
- The treating dentist
- The practice recall system (informing patients that they are due for a check-up).

All appointments made by the dental nurse should be made when they are convenient for both the patient and the treating dentist.

Appointment systems within the practice can be either manual or electronic. Both systems can be equally well adapted and implemented. Each system should include the name of the dentist, the date, the time of each appointment, the patient's name and the type of treatment to be carried out. This allows the dentist and other members of the dental team to know which patients will be attending the practice and what treatment is required.

Receptionists will use this information to prepare the patient notes, radiographs, laboratory work, etc. They will also be able to prepare a 'day sheet' which will be given to the nurse, before the beginning of the clinical session, enabling both the nurse and the dentist to see which patients will be attending the session, what time they will be attending, and what treatment is required.

Often 'free appointments' are kept on the appointment system for each day. This allows any patients who are in pain to be seen straight away. If additional patients are booked in all these 'free appointments', it will be the responsibility of the reception staff to inform the dentist and the dental nurse that the appointment has now been filled and to supply them with the details of the patient who will be attending and their notes.

Communicating with patients when making appointments

Dental appointments can be made by several methods.

Face to face

Patients will report to reception to make appointments for various reasons:

- ongoing dental treatment
- a scheduled check-up
- if they are in any pain
- if they need to re-schedule an appointment.

At all times the dental nurse should greet the patient suitably. Allow the patient enough time to explain what they require. Ask the patient when they would prefer to attend, see when the dentist is available and offer suitable appointments that are acceptable to both the patient and the treating dentist.

The dental nurse then needs to enter the patient's name and treatment required in the appointment system, and fill in the appointment details on the appointment card, which will be given to the patient. The dental nurse will also need to enter the appointment details in the patient notes.

Telephone

When making appointments for patients over the telephone it is essential that dental nurses answering the telephone state the name of the practice and ask how they may help the patient. Allow enough time for the caller to state their request, without interrupting them. If for any reason a patient needs to be put 'on hold' on the telephone system explain that this is being done. When discussing sensitive or personal information with the patient on the telephone a nurse must ensure that patients in the waiting room, or around the reception area, cannot overhear.

Again appointments should be made at a convenient time for the patient and when the dentist is available. The dental nurse should clearly inform the patient of the time and date of their appointment, and fill in an appointment card, with details of the appointment. The patient's address should also be checked and amended if necessary. Again, the scheduled appointment should be entered in the patient notes.

Letter

A dental practice will often inform patients of changes to their dental appointments or recall patients for a routine check-up by sending the patient a letter or pre-printed appointment card. Most dental practices operate a recall system that highlights when each patient is due for a check-up.

It is very important that the patient's home address details are checked and kept up to date to ensure that any correspondence reaches the patient. All information in letters or on pre-printed cards should be clearly stated. When sending appointments or letters to children ensure that the correspondence is addressed to the parent or guardian.

It is also important to track all recall appointments sent to patients. If patients fail to attend recall appointments, then they will need to be contacted again.

Electronically

When contacting a patient by either fax or e-mail, it is important to be aware that other people besides the patient may be able to read the information that you are sending. It is therefore important to limit the information that is sent – simply ask the patient to contact the dental practice to arrange an appointment.

Taking payments from patients

When working on reception the dental nurse will be expected to take and reconcile payments from patients for their dental treatment. It is therefore essential that the dental nurse understands:

- The practice's current charges for dental treatment
- The different methods of payments acceptable within the practice
- How to prepare estimates for dental treatments
- NHS entitlements and exemptions from changes.

At the beginning of each course of treatment, each NHS patient is required to complete an NHS 'Practice Record Form – Patient Declaration' (Fig. 17.1). This form acts as both a contract between the patient and the dentist, and written consent. Part A and part B of the form must be completed by the patient, or by someone else on behalf of the patient, before the course of dental treatment commences. All those patients who are exempt from paying NHS dental charges should complete part B of the form. Each patient who is exempt needs to complete the section of the form that applies to them. Patients will need to be asked to supply proof of their right to exemption. Patients at the end of their dental treatment will need to complete part C of the form. These forms are retained in the dental practice, unless requested by the Dental Practice Board.

It, therefore, follows that the dental nurses need to be fully aware of how and when to complete the required NHS paperwork.

It will be the dental nurse's responsibility and duty to inform patients of charges for their present course of treatment. This is calculated on the basis of the patient's treatment plan and notes on completed dental treatment. Using the practice dental charges for each item of treatment, the nurse should total the amount of money necessary to pay for the completed course of treatment.

Once the patient has been informed of the amount required to pay the bill in full, the dental nurse should inform the patient about the various methods of payment. These include:

- Cash
- Cheque
- Credit card.

Fig. 17.1 Patient completing NHS form.

The patient's payment is then recorded in both their notes and the patients' payment book. The patient's name, the date, amount paid and method of payment are recorded. After this the payment should be stored in a cash register, secure cash tin or a locked drawer.

As part of practice procedures, all patients should be issued with a receipt showing the date, patient's name and amount paid. Receipt stubs are kept as a record that a receipt has been issued.

Obvious responsibilities are involved when handling money, cheques and credit card payments. It is therefore essential that the dental nurse closely follow the dental practice procedures when taking payments. We are all human and mistakes can occur, so it is very important that, if you feel that you have made a mistake, you tell a senior member of staff immediately.

Reconciling patient payments

At the end of each clinical session or the working day it is essential that all patient's payments taken are checked, counted and processed. It will be the responsibility of the dental nurse to count all patient's payments taken and total the amount of cash, cheques and credit card payments against entries in the patient's payment book and payment receipts issued.

The amount of monies taken should balance the paying-in details and receipts issued. If there are any discrepancies the figures need to be checked again. Another responsible member often re-checks the patient's payment details, monies taken and receipts issued, as a safeguard that fraud or theft has not taken place. This system protects the members of staff handling the payments.

All cheques, credit card payment slips and monies are now removed from the till or cash tin and given to the practice manager or practice principal, who will store it securely until it is paid into the bank. Often only the practice principal and the practice manager are aware of the safe or safety box combination. It is usually the responsibility of the practice manager or practice principal to bank patient's payments. They will ensure that money is suitably prepared and paying-in slips completed before banking.

Many dental practices do not allow members of staff to take money from the till, even if it is to pay for stationery, etc. This ensures that all money is accounted for. All dental practices will have a procedure to deal with theft or fraud and it is vital that, if you feel that either has taken place, you inform the practice manager or practice principal straight away. Failure to do so could have serious consequences for all those involved.

18 Conscious Sedation

18: Conscious Sedation

Reasons for using sedation in dentistry

Conscious sedation has many benefits as opposed to general anaesthesia. As the name applies, the patient is aware of sounds and movements around them, but their level of anxiety is reduced. Patients are sedated for many reasons in many medical and dental situations (Table 18.1), and also where general anaesthesia is unfavourable. This may be because the patient:

- Has a disability that does not allow the completion of the dental procedure
- May be phobic with regard to dental procedures
- May retch during dental procedures.

Table 18.1 Actions and clinical indications of sedation

ACTION	CLINICAL INDICATIONS
Relief of anxiety	Anxiety and panic disorders, phobias
Promotion of sleep	Insomnia
Muscle relaxation	Muscle spasms and related disorders
Stopping fits, convulsions	Fits due to drug poisoning, some forms of epilepsy
Impairment of short-term memory	Pre-medication for operations, sedation for surgical procedures

Before sedation, the dentist will have to assess the patient's suitability, both medically and psychologically, to decide what type of sedation will be suitable. The patient has to sign a consent form and should have understood completely which procedure he or she is to undertake (**informed consent**) and that a complete medical and dental history has been taken. The latter includes:

- Allergies
- Reactions to anaesthetics – including history of family reactions
- General health
- Past operations
- Pregnancy
- Reason for preferring sedation
- Whether the patient has an escort for the return journey and also to stay with for the next 24 hours and, in the case of children, whether they be taken care of by another person.

On the day of the procedure, the general health is assessed again, including any minor illnesses, such as a blocked nose, particularly if the patient is having inhalational sedation, and it is checked that the consent form has been signed. The patient's blood pressure is taken, using a **sphygmomanometer**, before and throughout the duration of the procedure. A pulse oximeter is also used to monitor the level of oxygen in the patient's blood.

Intravenous sedation

When intravenous sedation is used, metered doses (titration) of the sedative agent are used and monitored on specific equipment, which will inform the operator how much sedative is used throughout the procedure, and also when the patient is likely to regain full consciousness. Agents used for intravenous sedation include midazolam (trade name Hypnovel), and come under the category of **benzodiazepines** (see below). Other sedatives include temazepam, chloral hydrate, nitrazepam and diazepam.

Benzodiazepines work by enhancing the actions of one of the natural brain chemicals that transmit messages from one brain cell to another. They help the messages to slow down, or stop firing, and quieten the reactions of these cells. As a result, anxiety is greatly reduced and muscles are more relaxed. The dentist can then complete the treatment as planned. A side effect is that short-term memory is impaired (amnesia). The drugs should be administered slowly, as respiratory depression can occur with rapid infusion.

Instruments and medications used for intravenous sedation

- Pulse oximeter (Fig. 18.1)
- Sphygmomanometer (Fig. 18.2)
- Stethoscope (Fig. 18.3)
- Monitoring equipment
- Syringe/cannula (Fig. 18.4)
- Sedative agent (Fig. 18.5)
- Reversal agent (antagonist), ie flumazenil (Fig. 18.5)
- Oxygen (Fig. 18.6)
- Emergency box.

Fig. 18.1 Pulse oximeter.

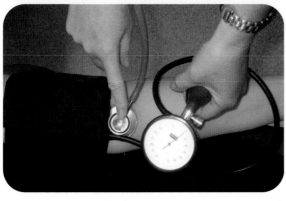

Fig. 18.2
Sphygmomanometer.

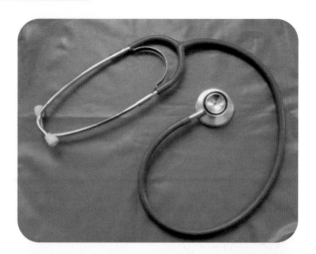

Fig. 18.3 Stethoscope.

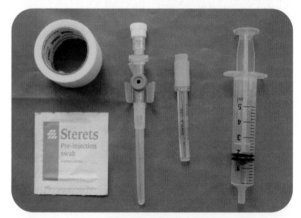

Fig. 18.4 Syringe and cannula. From left to right: surgical tape, alcohol wipe, venflon needle, syringe needle, syringe.

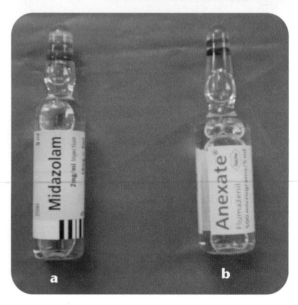

Fig. 18.5 (a) Sedative (midazolam) and (b) antagonistic (flumazenil) drugs.

Fig. 18.6 Oxygen cylinders. Left, nitrous oxide and right, oxygen.

Oral sedation

Oral sedation, such as diazepam, can also be used if the patient is particularly anxious about attending for treatment. This comes under pre-medication, and can be used either on its own or with other forms of sedation.

Inhalational sedation

For inhalational sedation a mixture of nitrous oxide (also referred to as happy gas) and oxygen is used. The ratio of nitrous oxide to oxygen depends on the depth of sedation that is required. The level of sedation also depends on whether or not the patient is mouth breathing, as this will dilute the strength, which is also why it is relevant that the patient can breathe adequately through their mouth. The quantity is usually at a minimum of 30% nitrous oxide (N_2O).

Instruments and medications used for inhalational sedation

- Pulse oximeter
- Sphygmomanometer
- Monitoring equipment
- Reversal agent
- Oxygen/nitrous oxide/halothane
- Relative analgesia machine (Fig. 18.7)
- Emergency kit (see Chapter 3, Fig. 3.1 and 'Contents of emergency kit' on p. 280)
- Mouth prop
- Scavenging equipment/correct ventilation
- Nasal mask (correct size(s)) (Fig. 18.8).

Fig. 18.7 Relative analgesia machine.

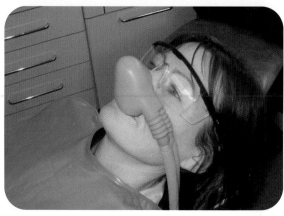

Fig. 18.8 Nasal mask in place.

Stages of sedation

There are four stages of 'twilight' conscious sedation:

- Minimal
- Moderate
- Deep
- General anaesthesia.

Minimal sedation

This is also known as anxiolysis, where patients can respond to verbal commands. Their coordination may be impaired, but their cardio-vascular functions remain unaffected.

Moderate sedation

This is also known as procedural sedation, and is more drug induced to allow the patients to respond purposefully, but with little stimulation required. The airway should be maintained without any intervention in this stage of sedation.

Deep sedation

With this depth of sedation, patients are not easily aroused, and it may be difficult to achieve any response. Patients may require airway maintenance in this stage (as with general anaesthesia). It may be suitable for patients undergoing prolonged and uncomfortable and/or painful procedures.

General anaesthesia

The patient is totally unconscious and their airway needs to be kept open by intubation and ventilation. They will not respond to any commands. General anaesthesia is used for prolonged and uncomfortable and/or painful procedures.

Risks associated with conscious sedation

There are few risks associated with conscious sedation, but you should always be prepared in the event the following:

- If an infusion is delivered too quickly the patient can go into respiratory arrest, and will require intubation and resuscitation if breathing stops altogether.

- If the patient has consumed alcohol within 24 hours of the procedure, the same (as above) can occur. The combination of the two drugs can have the same affect.

- Pregnancy/general health/sickle cell anaemia – the anaesthetist should be informed, so extra care can be taken.

- Instruments dropped down the patient's airway – care should be taken, as always, to keep the airway as clear as possible, and have suction equipment ready in the event of this happening.

- Low blood saturations – a pulse oximeter will alert you if the saturations drop below/between 95/100.

Contents of emergency kit

- Reversal drugs for intravenous sedation
- Adrenaline (epinephrine) – to treat anaphylactic shock
- Guedel airways (used for 'mouth-to-mouth' resuscitation)
- Suction tips
- Facemasks (to use with oxygen)
- Syringes/needles/cannulas
- Resuscitation drugs
- Cricothyrotomy kits (used when the airway is completely obstructed, and this is the only way to provide air into the lower part of the larynx).

Other emergency equipment

- Defibrillators
- Monitoring equipment
- Oxygen machine.

All staff should be well versed in what is expected of them if a patient's heart stops beating, or what to do when a respiratory arrest happens. See Chapter 3 for details.

THE DENTAL NURSE'S ROLE IN THE DIFFERENT STAGES OF CONSCIOUS SEDATION

Before sedation

- Retrieve the patient notes and identify the procedure.

- Check that patient's medical history in accordance with the procedure that they are having. It is alright for the patient to have eaten and or had a drink up to about two hours before, but not alcohol as this can mix dangerously with the sedation, causing respiratory suppression.

- Be aware of health and safety at all times and provide personal protective equipment for all staff and patients, to help minimise cross-infection, and aspirate when required.

- The patient should be asked to visit the toilet and loosen any tight clothing, such as a collar or belt.

- The patient's weight and blood pressure are taken; the blood pressure will be monitored throughout the procedure.

- All instruments, materials and medications should be ready and placed out of sight of the patient. The sedation equipment, such as cannulas, sedation and reversal drugs, oxygen and emergency kit should be well prepared, along with the aspiration equipment, which should be checked beforehand to ensure that it is in good working order.

- It is also important to have mouth props ready, as the patient's mouth will relax during the sedation and will need to be adequately supported to allow a clear airway, and also for the operator to be able to see what he or she is doing.

- Once the patient is settled into the dental chair, the anaesthetist will be able to prepare the injection site for the sedation to be administered. The dental nurse's role is to support the patient and promote a calm environment. You will need to remain in the room for the entire procedure – this is a legal requirement. A patient can sometimes hallucinate when undergoing sedation and, legally, you are required to be present, as a witness as well as a nurse.

- Be able to anticipate the next stage of any given treatment, so that you can prepare and provide adequate and professional continuity in the treatment plan.

There should be minimal noise and talking, as the patient's sense of hearing will be the last to disappear and the first to reappear when waking. During conscious sedation, the patient will appear asleep, but will respond to verbal requests throughout.

On discharge

- Ensure that the patient's **observations** are right.

- If the patient has had a cannula placed, ensure that this has been removed.

- Ensure that the patient has an escort who understands all given postoperative instructions and what to do in the event of any further problems.

- Ensure that the patient is aware of any further appointments.

- Thoroughly clean and clear the instruments, medicaments and materials away.

- Wipe surfaces with isopropyl alcohol or similar.

- Sterilise as required in a regularly serviced autoclave – keeping clean and dirty instruments away from each other, as well as ensuring that dirty gloves from the previous procedure do not contaminate 'clean' gloves.

KEY TERMS

Conscious sedation	The induced sedative state in which a patient is not totally unconscious, but is responsive to requests from the operator
Phobias	Fears within a person
Monitoring equipment	Equipment used by the anaesthetist to determine the continuous health of the patient while sedated.
Sphygmomanometer	Monitoring equipment that is placed around the patient's arm to measure the blood pressure
Benzodiazepines	Collective name for the group of sedatives frequently used during conscious sedation
Pulse oximeter	Used to detect the amount of oxygen in the blood
Antagonist	Used to reverse the action of sedation.

19 Teamworking and Continuing Professional Development

19: Teamworking and Continuing Professional Development

As a dental nurse you will be part of a team, and need to be aware of the legislation and general rules that apply to dental practice. By keeping abreast of current issues and developments you will help in the smooth running of the practice. Legislation for practices and dental nurses has changed dramatically over the past few years, with continuing professional development (CPD) becoming a valuable asset for dentists and their nurses. This will be explained in more detail later in the chapter.

Team meetings are an invaluable part of your role, and are there to identify your strengths, weaknesses and areas to improve upon. Interests and priorities change over time, as do learning styles, and regular meetings will enable you to resolve problems and discuss any other issues.

Registration

You may have already heard about registration becoming essential for dental nurses. If you have not been working full-time and have had a career break, you can check the grandparenting clause that is now in place. Table 19.1 explains how this is applied: it relates roughly to how many hours you have previously worked. If you have clocked up approximately 1000 hours over a 5-year period, you will be eligible for registration. Should this not be the case for you, a new Access to Registration and Training (ART) course is now in place and covers the topics listed later. This is to help dental nurses ease back into the workplace, efficiently and with confidence. **Please note that ART will be run for only two years from when registration is in place.** After this time, the onus will be on dental nurses themselves to get a place on the dental nursing course to qualify.

Table 19.1 Days worked per week — target is 1000 hours (see colour key on p. 289)

	DAYS WORKED PER WEEK			
Number of years employed	1	2	3	4
1	52	104	156	208
2	104	208	312	416
3	156	312	468	624
4	208	416	624	832
5	260	520	780	1040
6	312	624	936	1248
7	364	728	1092	1456
8	416	832	1248	1664
9	468	936	1404	1872
10	520	1040	1560	2080

Table 19.1 Key

You do not have sufficient hours to qualify for registration, but may be able to apply for registration if you have a qualification that is recognised by the General Dental Council (GDC). You can access this information by going on the GDC website: www.gdc.uk.org

You have enough hours to qualify for registration within the initial two years of registration. Once this begins, you should contact the GDC for an application form.

You have sufficient hours, and will probably have between two and four years' experience. You may also be able to register under one of the ART routes (during the eligibility period of two years following the input of registration).

Provided that you have remained in employment, maternity leave, sick leave, holiday and days spent in continuing professional development, you can count this time towards your hours when referring to Table 19.1 (this route will be open during the two-year transitional period only). For further information contact: info@smile-on.com; here are some other useful telephone numbers and websites:

General Dental Council

- Tel no: 020 7887 3800
- E-mail: Communications@gdc.org.uk

British Association of Dental Nurses

- Tel no: 0125 333 8360
- Website: www.badn.org.uk

National Examination Board of Dental Nurses

- Tel no: 01253 778417
- E-mail: Info@nebdn.org

Topics covered in ART:

- Cross-infection control
- Cardiopulmonary resuscitation and medical emergencies
- Health and safety
- Ionising radiation
- Working with dentists and patients
- Continuing professional development
- Communication and teamworking/ethics/confidentiality/dealing with patients and handling complaints.

After qualifying

Once you have qualified, there are several postgraduate qualifications that are available for you to enrol on:

- Oral Health Education Certificate
- Dental Radiography courses
- Orthodontic Nurse
- Orthodontic Therapist
- Dental Sedation
- Advanced Life Support
- General Anaesthesia
- Dental Receptionist course
- BTec in Dental Management

There is also the combined Dental Hygienist and Therapist course, for which entry requirements are two A levels (grades A–C). Please remember that there are also places for dental nurses in the Army, the Royal Navy and the Royal Air Force, and further information can be found on the following websites:

- www.royal-navy.mod.uk
- www.army.mod.uk/medical/dental/index

Purpose of staff meetings

Staff meetings and reviews are there to share best practice for all staff members. They are also there for the following:

- To identify problems – before they escalate.

- To encourage CPD – this is important for all dental nurses and, apart from the aforementioned postgraduate courses, other informative and updating courses such as cardiopulmonary resuscitation (CPR) training days at your workplace, exhibitions and conferences can also count towards this.

- To identify and clarify job roles – your job description should be clarified, so that you are aware of what is required from you: disciplinary procedures, holidays, sick pay, your hours and rates of pay.

- To monitor changes – keeping alert in the workplace, and being aware of changes to do with health and safety, ideas for progression and how to improve your environment.

- To promote new ideas – do not keep these to yourself. If you have a good idea, speak up!

- To share experiences – you may have worked in a different practice, or have thought of new ways in which to show improvement.

- To review new legislation – be aware of new legislation. CPD will help enlighten you about this, as will reading dental magazines.

- To evaluate strengths/weaknesses/areas to improve upon – this is applied by reflective practice, such as staff appraisals and reviews. Personal development plans can be put into action, and reviewed at a later date. This is an excellent way to air any issues or ideas that you may have, and to discuss how you can promote best practice.

THE DENTAL NURSE'S ROLE IN TEAMWORKING

- Identify problems early, and bring them to the attention of either those who are concerned or someone whom you can initially approach confidentially.

- Share best practice ideas.

- Have regular team meetings.

- Clarify your roles and ensure that any changes are with the agreement and approval of your employer.

Index